ALL FOR tHE BEST
HOW GODSPELL TRANSFERRED FROM STAGE TO SCREEN

BY *Andrew Martin*
FOREWORD BY PAUL SHAFFER

ALL FOR THE BEST:
How GODSPELL TRANSFERRED FROM STAGE TO SCREEN
©2012 ANDREW MARTIN

ALL RIGHTS RESERVED.

No part of this book may be reproduced in any form or by any means, electronic, mechanical, digital, photocopying, or recording, except for in the inclusion of a review, without permission in writing from the publisher.

Published in the USA by:

BEARMANOR MEDIA
P.O. BOX 71426
ALBANY, GEORGIA 31708
www.BearManorMedia.com

ISBN-10: 1-59393-677-X (alk. paper)
ISBN-13: 973-1-59393-677-8 (alk. paper)

Printed in the United States of America.

COVER ILLUSTRATION BY BECQUE OLSON

BOOK DESIGN AND LAYOUT BY VALERIE THOMPSON

TABLE OF CONTENTS

ACKNOWLEDGMENTS **1**

INTRODUCTION BY THE AUTHOR **3**

FOREWORD BY PAUL SHAFFER **11**

PART ONE: PREPARE YE **17**

PHOTO GALLERY **55**

PART TWO: DAY BY DAY **93**

PART THREE: LEARN YOUR LESSONS WELL **117**

INDEX **149**

This book is dedicated to the memory of all the late lamented *Godspell*ians, especially:

Lamar Alford

Joseph Beruh

Brian Eatwell

Jack Fitzstephens

David Greene

David Haskell

Jeannie Lange Haskell

Merrell Jackson

Michael Kamen

Ben Kazaszkow

Jeffrey Mylett

Ellen Stewart

John-Michael Tebelak

Lynne Thigpen

Kenneth Utt

and

Gilda Radner

Acknowledgments

To Ben Ohmart, and BearManor Media, for taking a chance on a little-known film historian. And to BMM's right-hand lady Sandra Grabman, for being one part Ida Koverman, one part Della Street, and one part den mother. Not to mention Eila Mell, a most treasured friend for thirty years, who said, "You really ought to contact my publisher if you ever have a film history project. I think you'd be a great fit."

To Becque Olson, for so much help with the artwork, and for creating a cover illustration that sings with as much power as any song Stephen Schwartz has ever written.

To attorney and childhood pal Norman Williams, for possessing the heart of ten lions, the brain of ten Einsteins, and the patience of a hundred saints.

To Bruce Nash, for being a fount of information far more than he'd possibly realize, as well as very much one of the good guys.

To Roy Frumkes, for being the first person to say, "You should really consider writing about film history. Between your journalism skills, your impeccable memory, your eye for detail and how much you love the movies, you'd probably be great at it."

To Bob Ickes and Galina Espinoza, for being the first unofficial captains of the Andrew Martin Cheerleading Squad. And to Paul Rossen, Michael Pierce, Jeff Marquis and Michael Dixon, for always being front and center with their pom-poms and megaphones.

To Corbin Ross, Alice J. Kane, Benita McShan and Annelise C. Imgrund, for not only being the best writers I know but for making me believe I could print one letter on a page and have it read like Tolstoy.

To all of my Hatchlings and Usdanites, for endless and undying support and devotion.

To family friend and protector Jackie Kello, for all those hours of playing the *Godspell* cassette in her car when I was a child, and the fun times singing along at the top of our collective lungs. And the fact that she's always been right there with me on the journey, 'by my side,' as it were.

To my late lamented great-uncle Paul Aden, for instilling in me the fact that all dreams are like a garden, and need to be watered and fed and tended with utmost care if we want them to grow from simple seeds.

To Marlene Mandel, for always being there when I needed her most.

To Gary, for always telling me I could do it if I tried.

And to my cherished and wonderful mom, Janet S. Arnold, who turned our family onto *Godspell* in the first place, and never stopped believing.

Introduction
by the Author

About fifteen years ago from the time of this writing, my step-niece (who has since grown into quite the picturesque example of womanhood, and goes by the first name of Danielle) asked her grandmother (my stepmother at the time), "Mom-mom, when you were a little girl, how many CDs did you have?" My stepmother laughed and said, "Dani, when I was a little girl, we didn't have CDs." To which Dani's big beautiful eyes grew even bigger, and she asked horrifically, "You mean music wasn't *invented* yet?"

At the time, of course, I thought this was adorable, as would any uncle and/or godfather without children, who chooses to live vicariously through the precious little ones in our lives. But as I creep closer and closer to middle-age (I may already be there, but I refuse to call it that or acknowledge such a thing), I'm amazed by the cultural perceptions of the young. Quite often I'll go to an entertainment-industry party and fall into conversation with some new starlet barely in their twenties and already halfway towards fame and fortune who, upon hearing my age, will say, "You mean you were actually born *before* the original *Woodstock*? What was that like??" I usually reply in deadpan, "Oh, it wasn't so bad. My folks had a very nice cave in Central Queens, and as long as we avoided the T-Rex, we were fine." Or, as happens much more frequently, "You mean, you actually remember a time when there was *no* MTV? What did you watch instead?" To which I say, "We didn't watch anything. We were too busy staring at the fire and dragging women around by their hair. It was our way of going clubbing."

The reason I open with this, in an Introduction which I'd sincerely hoped would be free of self-reference and has already failed miserably on that score after barely two paragraphs, is because I'd like to speak about musical education and the overwhelming importance thereof. I don't mean learning an instrument, although that's equally monumental. I mean exposing children to eclectic and wide-reaching musical taste at a very young age. This is equally important with literature or any other area of the creative and performing arts. But I'd like to concentrate here on opening the mind of a child to as many forms of music as possible, and why that's so very beneficial in the long run.

I was extremely fortunate to have been raised in a home where music in a variety of genres was lifeblood to both parents. My dad, Ken, exposed us all from a very early age to both sides of the entire 1950s catalog; on the one side there were the vocal stylings of Rosemary Clooney, Guy Mitchell, Doris Day, Tony Martin, Dinah Shore, Patti Page and Frankie Laine. On the other was doo-wop and nothing but doo-wop; the Coasters, the Drifters, the Orlons, the Tokens, Freddie 'Boom-Boom' Cannon, and Danny and the Juniors. Sometimes a happy medium was reached, as in the case of the Four Lads. And in the car, all that ever played on the radio were the current pop hits of the time in the mid-1970s, which gave an exposure to Barry Manilow, Carly Simon, Diana Ross and Paul McCartney among others, not to mention the very beginnings of disco and also such wonderful artists as Andrew Gold and Dorothy Moore.

My mother Janet, meanwhile, who very much enjoyed the music of the 1950s and as a teenager was particularly a fan of the jazz legend Dakota Staton, made sure that her children were far more musically enriched than anything my dad could accomplish; because of her, we were consistently exposed to a mix of classical music, including such operatic pieces as *Carmina Burana* and *La Boheme* besides all the great violinists (Heifetz, Rabin, Neveu, etc), cantorial recordings by Moyshe Oysher, the Kadima Singers and the Barry Sisters, the occasional pop album by Barbra Streisand, Bette Midler or Simon & Garfunkel, French pop music by the likes of Jacques Brel and Edith Piaf, such jazz artists as Stephane Grappelli, everything ever written or recorded by Noel Coward, and such international artists as Miriam Makeba. In fact, the only true common ground I knew my parents to share was a mutual love of Ella Fitzgerald, whose concert they attended at Forest Hills Stadium in the early 1960s shortly after they were married. Although, they also dearly loved the music-comedy recordings of Allan Sherman and Tom Lehrer, and owned every album by both.

And then, there were show tunes. Now, when I say that, I know the mind immediately jumps to the likes of Rodgers & Hammerstein, Lerner & Loewe, Cole Porter, Frank Loesser, Jule Styne and Stephen Sondheim. Not so in our home in Rego Park. The very first show album to which I ever knew all the words, because it played constantly on the stereo from my infancy, was *Jacques Brel is Alive and Well and Living in Paris*. Another was *Hair*. A third, slightly more traditional, was *The Rothschilds*, and there were also the film soundtracks from *Fiddler on the Roof* and *Sweet Charity* besides the London recording of *Stop the World, I Want to Get Off*. But the one that may have played more than any of them was *Godspell*. I didn't completely understand what it was about, and my parents, being Conservative Jews, didn't much take the time to explain the New Testament. But I did know, even before I started kindergarten, that it was one of my favorite records and I could never tire of listening to it.

Then one day when I was eight years old or thereabouts, I was in my parents' room watching television by myself on a Sunday afternoon (this was, of course, back in the days when there were only thirteen stations and no remotes, so "channel-surfing" involved the now-primitive task of standing at the set and flipping the dial until finding something worth catching). When I got to Channel 5 (which was then WNEW-TV in New York), I was incredibly surprised to see a bunch of grownups splashing around in a fountain in the city in their clothes, singing "Prepare Ye, The Way of the Lord." That was the first time I ever realized that *Godspell* was also a movie. I very excitedly ran to the living room, where my mother was enjoying a live broadcast of a Bruch concerto on WQXR Radio, and exclaimed, "*Godspell*'s on TV!! It's a movie!! Did you know it's a movie?" She said, "Yes, I know it's a movie. Dad and I went to see it when you were little. I'm listening to this right now, but go on in and watch." I went back and sat on the bed, riveted to the screen, scarcely believing that I was able to put faces to the voices; one memory that strikes me at this writing was the angelic visage of Robin Lamont, perched atop the hood of a truck, singing "Day by Day." Once again I didn't fully understand what it was about, and I also remember being somewhat afraid of some of the action, like Lamont's 'descent into Hades' with the demons pouring ketchup onto strawberry cream pies, and of course the Pharisee Monster's deep scary voice. And at one point I had to run back down the hall and ask my mom, "Why are they having a Seder?" to which she replied, "It's because Jesus was Jewish. I know, that may sound confusing, but I'll explain it all to you later. Go back and watch." So I did, and by the end, when they all disappeared into the city and the streets were suddenly once again alive with people, I was mystified. We all know that an eight-year-old, no matter how vaguely savvy, can't possibly be a great judge of cinematic brilliance, but the film left me absolutely thunderstruck. And from that day on, as I listened to the album with more and more personal enthusiasm (which still hasn't ebbed for a moment), I never missed a broadcast of the movie. The day we got our first VCR years later was joyous enough, but then to be able to record *Godspell* from Channel 9 (WOR-TV) and watch it whenever I wanted, was truly a fantasy realized.

By my early twenties, while continuing to pursue my career as an entertainer, I suddenly fell backwards into a sideline in journalism, writing reviews of theater and music besides feature articles and interviews, as well as broadcasting in both radio and television. I've been juggling both onstage and offstage appearances for over two decades, and it's simply the work I've chosen for myself. But I do confess to being occasionally starstruck; the thing is, whereas other people might be starstruck about encountering a Paul Newman or an Elizabeth Taylor, I get starstruck over, as a dear friend of mine once put it, 'people nobody ever heard of.' Which, I suppose is true; certain people make an impact on me and I immediately tend to place them within an artistic plateau that staggers my mind. All of the original cast of *Godspell* and those who appeared in the movie are no exception. It was, therefore, an incredible experience in 1990 when I was asked to interview the four cast members of a small musical revue called *Songs in Blume*, all penned by a late composer named Bobby Blume, and was informed that among them would be Peggy Gordon. Peggy Gordon? *Godspell* Peggy Gordon? 'By My Side' Peggy Gordon?? *PEGGY GORDON*?? Even weak in the knees as I was from this, I managed to stroll into the Duplex and confidently interview them all, but I never once took my eyes off of Peggy, and I'm loathe to admit that I paid more attention to her in the interview than any of the others (who, for the record, were three sensational performers named Michael McAssey, Amy Ryder, and the late lamented Michael Callan). I had the opportunity to meet her two years later, at the one-man show of a mutual composer-friend of ours named John Forster, but though I greeted her with extreme eagerness, she barely remembered who I was. Which didn't offend me; after all, this was PEGGY GORDON. Since that time, I also had the chance to become acquainted with Robin Lamont and with *Godspell*'s original stage manager Nina Faso, and was privileged to enjoy some short special moments with Lynne Thigpen before her unexpected passing, as well as briefly meeting Jerry Sroka at an event along with his lovely wife, Mariette Hartley. I even got to meet Stephen Schwartz once in 2001, when he and I both attended a Jane Olivor concert at the Westbury Music Fair. And every time, what echoed constantly in my brain was, "It's a *Godspell* person! You met an actual *Godspell* person!!"

Now we jump to the very recent past of 2011. Momentarily finding myself without a print or Internet venue in which to write my reviews and feature articles, I launched my blog, The Andrew Martin Report, on Wordpress.com. Once it was announced that *Godspell* would be returning to Broadway at the Circle in the Square Theater, a light bulb went off over my head and I contacted Robin Lamont, asking if I could possibly do an interview with her, sort of a commemoration of *Godspell*'s fortieth anniversary and to celebrate the show's return. Though she's very busy with her home life and her new career of writing suspense novels (and, as an aside, her debut book *If Thy Right Hand* is a must-read), she agreed and we set the wheels in motion. A few days later, she contacted me and said, "I hope you don't mind, but I was having lunch with Peggy Gordon and Sonia Manzano, and I mentioned the interview we'll be doing, so they were wondering if they could also be included." Well, no one has to twist my arm to ever expand an article, much less something I've written about *Godspell*, so of course I told her that would be fine. She replied, "That's great, because Gilmer McCormick wants to be in it, too." Now my head was spinning. *Four* of the original women of *Godspell*? Well, my inner Louella Parsons must have kicked into overdrive, because I contacted Nina Faso, explained all of this to her, she put me in touch with JJ McCraty (formerly known as Joanne Jonas), and before I knew it I was interviewing all six of them. It was the first time anyone has ever written solely of the original women of the company; up until now, it had always been as individuals or with the entire cast. I did the best I could with it, published it on August 2, and figured that maybe it might net some small semblance of a reaction if I was fortunate.

Next, not only was the blog receiving hundreds of hits, but someone of importance asked if I would entertain the idea of expanding it somewhat into a book about the making of the film? And if so, could it be done quickly? Well, I've never been one to turn down a challenge, so I said yes. My first step was to immediately re-establish contact with all six women as well as Jerry Sroka, and ask if they'd be opposed to being interviewed again for a book. All not only responded with enthusiasm, but promptly connected me to Stephen Schwartz, Edgar Lansbury, Victor Garber, Katie Hanley, Susan Tzu and Stephen Reinhardt (which wasn't altogether unconquerable, since he also happens to have been Gilmer's husband since the earliest days of *Godspell*). On my own, I managed to find Sammy Bayes, Alan Heim, and Nicolas Greene. And my cherished friend Robert Patrick filled me in with some anecdotes about what he knew of the show and the people involved. In addition, Peggy managed to put me in touch with Paul Shaffer, who so very graciously consented to write the Foreword. Thus, the book you are reading now, which came together possibly even more quickly than Tebelak's original script (Robin even asked me, several days before submitting the manuscript, "How on earth did you manage to write this all so quickly?"). It has emerged both a spectacular challenge and a labor of love of which I couldn't possibly be more proud, and which I conversely and fervently hope will serve as a beacon for anything I might accomplish in the future.

The moral of the story, and especially for any expectant mothers and fathers who are out there reading this, is to please, *please* be sure to educate your children as broadly as possible about all forms of music. Because, honestly, what you're reading here is what could very well be result of providing them with such a wondrous cultural foundation, the way my parents did for me and so many other parents have done for theirs. As Stephen Schwartz once wrote, and St. Matthew long before him, let your light so shine before men.

Enjoy the book, enjoy *Godspell*, and thank you for your time and attention.

ANDREW MARTIN
NEW YORK CITY
SEPTEMBER 2011

Foreword
by Paul Shaffer

I tell you this: a long, long time ago, in the early 1970s, there was a show called *Godspell*, which had been a hit in New York and Los Angeles and was now coming to Toronto, where I happened to have gone to college. I knew a lovely young actress who wanted to audition for it, and she asked if I would accompany her on piano. The song she chose was from the show— "Bless the Lord"— and we learned it together from the original cast album. Even though I took piano lessons as a kid, sight-reading isn't my strong suit and I'm much better off if I can learn a song by hearing it a few times. So we went to the audition. The team that was handling the casting included the show's composer, Stephen Schwartz. Not only was the actress offered a job on the spot, but so was I. Maybe I was very young or very talented, or a combination of both, or maybe neither. All I know is that Schwartz, who was also maybe very young and very talented, and certainly both, heard something in the way I played his tune that made him say, "Would you play for the remainder of the auditions? I like your musical style better than our guy." At the end of the day, he spoke to me again. "Can you get a band together and conduct this show for me?" This was unprecedented. I'd been 'discovered,' like Lana Turner at Schwab's.

The thing about Stephen Schwartz is that even though he's a theatrical composer, he very much has a rock sensibility, and he and I are both very similar in that way. We both loved Elton John and Laura Nyro, and I think you can hear these influences in the *Godspell* music. Maybe that's what Stephen appreciated in my playing. At any rate, I was thrilled to take the gig, my first real job in show business.

One of the first people I met once I was hired officially was Stephen Reinhardt. He had already musically directed the show Off-Broadway where it first became a hit, and then in Los Angeles, Boston, and some cities in Europe. Aside from supervising, and brilliantly, the way all the music would be executed for these companies, he also served as the choreographer because he'd been a dancer on Broadway. Our cast, which was stupendous, included Victor Garber as Jesus, as well as Martin Short, Eugene Levy, Andrea Martin, and Gilda Radner. I naturally gravitated towards these funny kids, and became great friends with all of them. Soon after we opened, we heard the news that Victor had been cast in the film version. We were all elated.

Of course Victor left the show at that point, and was replaced temporarily by Don Scardino. Then Donny was replaced by Gordon Thomson, who many remember as Adam Carrington on *Dynasty* in the mid-1980s. Finally, Gordon was replaced by Eugene Levy, who played the Herb Braha role originally, but was really ideally suited to play Jesus because of his singing voice. He would have gotten the role at the beginning except, well, frankly, Eugene is a very hairy guy. At the top of the first act, after everyone is baptized by John, Jesus appears in a pair of swim trunks for his own baptism. When Eugene took over the role, they made him add a tank top for the matinees. Perhaps they thought a hirsute Jesus might 'scare the kids.' But it all worked out, because at that point Dave Thomas took over the Herb role, and became a key friend of ours. Of course, Marty, Eugene, Dave and Andrea all went on to great success with *SCTV*. And to this day, whenever Eugene, Marty, Dave and I get together, which is often, we always sing the entire *Godspell* score from top to bottom. It's our ritual. The show had such an impact on our young adulthood that we don't need sheet music or anything—we just remember it.

Then, of course, there was Gilda Radner. You couldn't help but love her. She came into the role created in New York by Gilmer, and at her audition, singing "Zip-a-Dee-Doo-Dah," she was so cute she was breathtaking. I got to work with her again later, not just on *Saturday Night Live*, but also on her Broadway show *Gilda Radner: Live from New York* at the Winter Garden Theater, for which she and I collaborated on the songs. I realize now that those numbers, like "I Love To Be Unhappy" and "Honey, Touch Me With My Clothes On," certainly have a *Godspell*-like sensibility. How could they not? This was where we both began.

Jumping back to 1972, I got a phone call to come to New York and play keyboards on the film soundtrack of *Godspell*. This was in part because Steve Reinhardt really wanted me involved, for which I'll always be grateful, and also because Stephen Schwartz felt that what I brought to the music, a little lick here and there, added something to the score. After all, I had learned these songs by ear, and in some cases, put my own spin on them. Getting to New York was like something out of a movie, too. There was an airport workers' strike in Toronto, so after our Sunday performance, I had to catch a bus to Buffalo and then fly down. New York thrilled and amazed me, seeing all the brownstone houses I'd only ever known from the movies. I went directly to the rehearsal hall on 52nd Street. Across the street there was the Cheetah, that Latin dance club I'd heard so much about. Every restaurant had pictures of celebrities on the walls. I was in heaven. The next morning, I emerged from my hotel, got in a cab and told the driver to take me to the recording studio at 799 7th Avenue, which turned out to be across the street. I sheepishly got out, and walked back to the studio.

All three of the original guys from the *Godspell* band, Jesse Cutler, Richie LaBonte and Ricky Shutter, were there because Stephen Schwartz wanted to retain the marvelous instrumental sound of the original cast album. Schwartz and Reinhardt worked perfectly together—they were as one. And there were other musicians too, really good sessions guys who were a pleasure to work with. I remember Michael Kamen, a great musician who died a few years ago after tremendous success in the industry, playing a screech on the ARP 2600 synthesizer when the Pharisee Monster loses an eye in the "Alas For You" scene. And, the studio had a direct line to Wolf's Deli. If I suddenly wanted a corned beef sandwich in the middle of the session, I could have one. Me, this nobody kid from Canada. Who knew?

On the third day, Schwartz and I worked on underscoring. One section involved a parable told in silent-movie clips, and accompanied appropriately. To rehearse this, I went two evenings in a row, all alone, to the Lansbury/Duncan/Beruh office at 1650 Broadway, an extremely important address in New York entertainment, and practiced all night on Edgar Lansbury's grand piano. I must say that all the *Godspell* people, Lansbury, Beruh, and everyone else on down, were genuinely nice and so generous. Could the Biblical nature of the show have had anything to do with this? I think so. In any case, the underscoring was put on tape, sometimes with Stephen Schwartz and me on dual pianos. I then returned to Toronto to continue playing the stage show, but I was never the same. I vowed to someday return to New York.

When the movie was released in Toronto, I went to see it with our cast at an afternoon showing. We thought it was lovely, a very effective way of bringing the show to the screen. But I did notice that the theater was half-empty, and couldn't figure out why. Maybe it was because *Jesus Christ Superstar* was also playing at the time and had a bigger buzz. And I didn't much like that people were leaving as the credits rolled; after all, it was one of the first times in a film that all of the musicians for a soundtrack were actually listed in the crawl at the end. That my organ solo was screaming in accompaniment was an added thrill for me. So like I say, I really thought it was a hit. And then the reviews came out. I wish I'd published a couple myself—but that's what's makes horse races.

So here we are, all these years later, and you know what? It makes me happy that the movie still holds up. It's got a huge following. It plays on television every Easter. It was my first time in a New York recording studio, and the material was the wonderful *Godspell* soundtrack. Of this, I couldn't be more proud.

"Make a joyful noise unto the Lord, all the earth; make a loud noise, and rejoice, and sing praise."
— *Psalms 98:4*

"Hey, Judy! Let's put on a show!"
— *Mickey Rooney*

PART ONE: PREPARE YE

The weather was warm and seasonable on the evening of May 17, 1971, and the small cul-de-sac of Commerce Street, in the western part of New York's Greenwich Village, had become suffused with the energy of a brand-new musical hit Off-Broadway, known as *Godspell*. As the opening-night audience left the historic Cherry Lane Theater in a state of jubilation, many of them humming the tuneful "Day by Day," the show's cast of ten were hurrying out of clown makeup and costumes while the band and crew collected themselves, in order to head to Sardi's en masse and wait for the first reviews. Sure enough, the show was a smash and a splendid time was had by all, save for cast member Gilmer McCormick, who suffered a severe gash to her foot on the cyclone fence during the climatic Crucifixion scene and had to be rushed to the emergency room for eight stitches, thereby missing the following two performances. And not every review was on *Godspell*'s side; Clive Barnes was his customary acerbic self in the *New York Times*, but gracious enough to admit that "the show will certainly attract an audience who will love it." (Interestingly, as stated by cast member Joanne Jonas, it was a short time thereafter when the show's producers took a full-page ad in the publication, quoting Barnes at the top, then captioning, "Right you are, Mr. Barnes!" and filling in the rest of the space with the raves the show had garnered). The original cast album was recorded six days later and sold like hotcakes, and *Godspell* had proven itself once and for all as the new feel-good entertainment of the season, thoroughly trouncing and all but eclipsing such other new rock-theater hits on and off-Broadway as *Hair, Jesus Christ Superstar, Salvation* and *Your Own Thing*. Which was in part a miracle and at the same time no surprise whatsoever, given the intricate journey the show had to travel to get there.

Godspell was the brainchild of John-Michael Tebelak, a plucky native of Ohio, who wrote the show in 1969 as his Master's thesis while a student at Carnegie-Mellon University in Pittsburgh. Based on the parables told within the Gospel According to St. Matthew, from the get-go it just had 'that thing' that seemingly foretold its success and deemed it worthy to go on to greater glory. The initial concept most largely borrowed from American Street Theater traditions and Commedia Dell'Arte besides broad vaudeville and slapstick, and featured a cast of clowns modeled on the great philosophers. And the rock-based score was composed by Duane Bolick, who would also provide musical direction and accompaniment along with his friend Captain Horton on organ. Casting one's own show might prove Herculean to some, but with so many to choose from among the world-renowned theater department of CMU, a larger problem for Tebelak was who to choose as opposed to who to omit, and in the end he opted to go with no performer with whom he'd worked before. The most notable of these were David Haskell as Judas/John the Baptist, a native of California's San Joaquin Valley, whose swarthy good looks, definitive presence and incredible voice for both speaking and singing made him an easy contender among classmates as the Most Likely To Succeed; Robin Lamont, a beautiful honey-blonde from Boston with a sultry folk-rock singing voice, and bouncy Sonia Manzano, a dazzling fireball of Puerto Rican descent who had come to Carnegie after graduating among the top of her class at New York's High School for the Performing Arts. He gave the remainder of the male roles to Andy Rohrer as Jesus besides Bob Ari, Stan King and Jamie Stevens, and for the women chose Randy Danson, Martha Jacobs and Mary Mazziotti. Tebelak would handle the staging, and stage management was provided by Nina Faso. Two other classmates, Susan Tzu and Lowell Achziger, designed the costumes and lighting respectively. "It was one of my first designs," said Tzu. "John-Michael wanted a set of costumes that incorporated both hippies and clowns. We *were* all hippies at the time, so that came naturally, and I guess the clown part did too!" And the cast, according to reports, by and large had a difficult time during the rehearsal process, mostly because they couldn't relate to what Tebelak was talking about in terms of vision. "The first time I met John-Michael, I was sure he was out of his mind," Robin Lamont said. Also, only a few (namely Haskell, Lamont and Manzano, and Rohrer, Ari and Danson more often than not) were true comedic actors, with the ability to do what Tebelak expected towards bringing his baby to life. However, through intense improvisation coupled with severe dedication and putting the show on its feet, word spread like wildfire throughout the Carnegie campus after the initial performances that something extremely exciting was being borne upon the school's long-hallowed stages.

It was very shortly thereafter, in early 1970, that Ellen Stewart became aware of the *Godspell* buzz when an associate at Carnegie gave her the alert, and she subsequently offered to bring the show to her LaMama Experimental Theater Company, in New York City's East Village. This was a momentous move for the show; Stewart and LaMama were already known far and wide as one of the most important cornerstones of the burgeoning Off-Off-Broadway scene that had begun to permeate the Big Apple's cultural landscape in the early 1960s, alongside such others as the Caffe Cino, and The Living Theater, which was governed by the husband-and-wife team of Julian Beck and Judith Malina. Charles Haid, a fellow theater student at CMU, was so enthusiastic about the show's potential that he came on board as an unofficial associate producer, helping the team make the move to New York and pledging his support to not only aid the transition as smoothly as possible, but do anything imaginable to assist in the show's success. However, the majority of the cast chose not to migrate to the city on such a gossamer wing and a prayer, and only Lamont, Haskell and Manzano came along for the ride as well as costume and lighting designers Tzu and Achziger.

From there, Tebelak hand-selected his cast from among college classmates with whom he'd worked previously and already had an established rapport. These included a tall, willowy brunette from New York named Peggy Gordon, who not only showed great promise as an actress and singer but had tremendous and innate skills as a composer; a slender, slightly-impish colleen named Gilmer McCormick from Louisville, Kentucky, who had no illusions of being an accomplished vocalist but possessed a tremendous sense of comic timing and dramatic ability; Jeffrey Mylett of Tebelak's native Ohio, a short pixie of a man with a blinding smile and dazzling talent not only as an actor-singer but as a musician; Herb Braha, a gentleman from Cape Cod of larger stature but with impeccable movement skills and ability for dialects, and bright-eyed Stephen Nathan, a native of Buffalo, who would become the new Jesus in Rohrer's place. Two other Carnegie classmates, Jimmy Canada and Prudence Wright Holmes, would also venture north from the Pittsburgh campus to join the fold. Bolick had also decided not to travel for this incarnation of the show, and so teaching the vocal portions of his score to the newer members of the cast most largely fell to Robin Lamont. For the band, Tebelak enlisted three teenaged brothers who were family friends from Ohio; eighteen-year-old Richard Quinn on keyboards, sixteen-year-old Marty on guitar, and fourteen-year-old Doug on percussion. (The three were delighted beyond words to be given a summer job away from home, were by all accounts excellent musicians besides very well-brought-up young men, and it was a sad occasion for all involved when they returned back home and to school).

The transition from college thesis-play to the mainstream wasn't easy, and stage manager Faso, who had already left Carnegie and had to be sent for by Tebelak, arguably felt it harder than anyone. "My mom called me in San Francisco when I was living there in 1970, and said, 'John-Michael has been looking all over for you, so you have to be in New York right away!!' I didn't ask any questions," she said. "I had heard about the show here and there, and that it was moving on to a bigger future, but I knew with our past that John-Michael really needed me. And I wanted to stay in San Francisco, but I had no money. My mother arranged for an airline ticket back east, and I soon found a place to live on Forsyth Street near Chinatown. I was young, scared, and horrified by the size of the city. But John-Michael gave me the script to read, and said we were going to do the show again, except that we wanted to spruce it up. When the cast members straggled in from Brooklyn, which is where many stayed with Robin Lamont, we did a full run-through for each other on my first day at LaMama, of what the show already was and would become. Ellen Stewart was there, and it was sort of a command performance for her and for each other. I loved what it had become and was moved by the show, and I thought it really was a great piece to do more work on.

"John-Michael was very sketchy, and kind of sloppy as a creator," she continued. "That's why he called me, of course, because I saw many places to expand. Some things *really* didn't work. But at its core, it was ten clowns, a fence, bags of garbage and a grotto setting. Which I thought was great for the show, to be contained in a grim and secular space, and burst out of it, like a cornucopia spilling the fruits of Christianity on a deaf and blind world in misery. That was my feeling about the nascent value of the show, and what I felt we had, at least in an embryonic form.

"We had an opening-night performance date looming at LaMama, and our rehearsal space was the loft John-Michael had been given for living and rehearsal. I stayed there and tried to keep him on track, and deal with mundane things. Like the script. So I was sort-of stage managing plus directing, and having just come from San Fran, I brought a lot of physical interest with me. John-Michael and I wanted to expand the parables without using fancy effects. We broke into groups and worked on specific pieces; we never gave too much thought to the aggregate effect. You see, we knew from the interest in the show that it had a glow. We did endless versions of just-as-many endless parables until we felt we had a decent and funny show, with a shape from Misery to Joy to the miracle of the Resurrection. I mostly left the music rehearsals and scheduling for that to Gilmer and Robin and Peg. They were our Three Marys, after all. And we had some facsimiles of Suzi Tzu's costumes from the original show. Other designers were around by that point, but I don't remember anything except the work, trying to keep the troops fed, and somehow finding a way to put up a fence at LaMama."

Cast member Jeffrey Mylett proved a pal indeed by throwing himself headfirst into helping Faso et al achieve anything that needed an extra hand. "God bless Jeffrey," Faso said, "for helping me constantly, to try to do crew work and act, too. He was brilliant. But we had so much to do. We had no money and no real producer, and the way some of it unfolded was just downright comical. One of my best memories was trying to rent a truck down in Lower

Manhattan, to move a chain-link fence from the ironyard to LaMama on the day before opening night. I didn't have a driver's license and Jeff had no money, so I think we used someone's parents' credit card and Jeffrey's Ohio license. We finally rented the truck, loaded the fence, and then picked up our garbage props and everything from my place on Forsyth Street. It took four of us to drive the truck; one for the steering, one for the clutch, one to shift; it was a nightmare! So we finally got to load-in at LaMama. We had no time for artistic concerns at this point; we just had to pitch in. And some of the cast was still learning lines and long speeches for the Prologue at the top of the show just hours before we opened." A collaborative effort, to be sure.

Well before this, Duane Bolick's score had been augmented somewhat. Peggy Gordon had written the music to a haunting ballad entitled "By My Side," for which fellow Carnegie student Jay Hamburger contributed the lyrics, and it was at Gilmer McCormick's persuasive insistence that the song find a place within the show, ultimately sung by Gordon with McCormick's harmony. Another hypnotic ballad, "The Raven and the Swan," had been written by Jeffrey Mylett and was sung by him with accompaniment on acoustic guitar; the lyrics provide perhaps the clearest glimpse of *Godspell* in its earliest incarnations, and how it tried to convey a combination of peace, love, understanding, religion and fun:

> *High above the treetops flies the Raven*
> *Down below on a looking-glass sea there floats the gentle Swan*
> *The Raven flies alone*
> *The Swan drifts on her own*
> *And yet they are quite together*
> *Unknowing birds of a feather*
> *The Raven and the Swan*
> *The Raven and the Swan*
> *The Raven and the Swan*
> *Together they are one*
> *Long before you opened your eyes, He spoke the Word*
> *For two eternities after you the Word will be heard*
> *The old become the young*
> *One plus one is one*

And so it goes on forever
Beads of life sprung on fine leather
The Raven is the Swan
The Raven is the Swan
The Raven is the Swan
It all goes on and on
Those of you who ask for explanation
Let it be said that Word is just creation
Creation, creation, creation, creation
Creation, creation, creation, creation
Creation, creation, creation, creation
Creation, creation, creation
The Raven and the Swan

Ready or not, here they came, and *Godspell* sprang forth at LaMama in 1970. Every performance ended with a standing ovation, even if the initial sold-out crowds (which included large tour groups from such faraway lands as Scandinavia and the Netherlands) thinned before long. The show did garner a cult following from the get-go, however, including the unerring attention of a young unknown thespian named Robert DeNiro, who attended constantly. Robert Patrick, a regular fixture at LaMama and one of the genre's most prolific and prodigious playwrights (he would later enjoy tremendous success when his play *Kennedy's Children* opened on Broadway at the John Golden Theater in 1975, starring Shirley Knight, Barbara Montgomery and Michael Sacks among others) saw that incarnation and said, "It wasn't drawing well at LaMama by that point. I saw it only because dear Ellen was standing in the doorway of the theater, stopped me as I passed on the street and begged me to go in and give it some audience. She said, 'It ain't much good, but they're good kids and they all worked hard to bring it up here from school.'" However, providence stepped in when the aforementioned Charles Haid invited Edgar Lansbury and producing partner Joseph Beruh to see the show, and the two, sensing a potential hit in the making, wasted no time in assuming the helm.

Lansbury and his twin brother Bruce were born into a family with impeccable theatrical lineage. Their mother was renowned stage actress Moyna MacGill, whose uncle was the legendary Scottish actor and producer Robert B. Mantell. Older sister Angela had been making an impact on film audiences ever since her scene-stealing debut in *Gaslight* in 1942, and later came into her own as a musical-comedy powerhouse in the title role of *Mame* on Broadway. In addition, he was the brother-in-law of Peter Ustinov, who was married to oldest sister Isolde, from MacGill's marriage to playwright/director Reginald Denham. His initial success came by way of television at CBS, as Art Director for the popular *The Red Skelton Hour* from 1954 through 1961, followed by the E.G. Marshall/Robert Reed series *The Defenders*, before embarking on career as a producer of the 1963 film *Star Witness*. A year later, he cast his eye towards Broadway by producing and also designing the sets for *The Subject Was Roses*, starring Jack Albertson and a then-unknown Martin Sheen; it went on to win the 1965 Tony Award for Best Play. Though the next several seasons contained professional disappointments for Lansbury where Broadway was concerned (with such plays as *That Summer – That Fall* and *The Only Game in Town* besides the never-officially-opened *A Way Of Life* in 1969, and the flop musical *Look To The Lilies*), he nonetheless maintained prestige as a producer for film and television, first with the series *Coronet Blue* and then the big-screen depiction of *The Subject Was Roses*, for which Jack Albertson won the 1968 Oscar for Best Supporting Actor.

Beruh couldn't have had more different a life and career than Lansbury; he was from solid middle-class Jewish stock in Pittsburgh, where his father owned a dry cleaning establishment. His initial ambition was to be an actor, and in 1951 first appeared off-Broadway in repertory with the Loft Players at the Circle in the Square Theater, before minor roles in Brecht/Weill's *The Threepenny Opera* at Theatre de Lys in 1954, and a Broadway debut in 1957's *Compulsion* at the Ambassador, for which he also served as stage manager. He'd also given directing a whirl, commandeering the 1953 summer season at the Grand Teton National Theater in Jackson Hole, Wyoming, as well as *A Sound of Hunting* at the Cherry Lane almost immediately thereafter. His first attempt at producing was a small revival of the 1920s musical *Leave it to Jane* at the Sheridan Square Theater in 1959, and *Kittiwake Island* at the Martinique a year after. But in 1961, he became one of New York's most successful General Managers for theater, when he took the driver's seat for *Elsa Lanchester, Herself* at the 41st Street and a string of other hits, mostly off-Broadway (although, in 1962, he also served as Company Manager for the musical smash *I Can Get It For You Wholesale* at the Shubert, which marked the show-stopping Broadway debut of a young Barbra Streisand). *The Subject Was Roses* was his first chance to work with Lansbury as a General Manager, both at the Royale Theater and the national tour that followed, and it would be one of several opportunities to develop together, which would last for nearly two successive decades. Their first full effort as producing partners was with 1969's *Promenade!* at the Promenade Theater, and by 1971 they'd added another partner, business whiz Stuart Duncan, with whom they produced the revival of Samuel Beckett's *Waiting for Godot* and the new play *Louis and the Elephant*, both at the Sheridan Square. They, as well as Duncan, felt that *Godspell* unquestionably had the raw beginnings of a hit, but also sensed that a crucial element was needed to make the proceedings fully realized. Enter composer Stephen Schwartz, another Carnegie alum, for whom they had been seeking the proper vehicle to showcase his astonishing compositional talents.

Schwartz, a native of Long Island who grew up in Williston Park, had already become something of a legend in his own time at Carnegie, having written music and lyrics for a little show called *Pippin*, and Nina Faso wasn't just a fan but a friend. "I first met Steve early in freshman year," she recalled. "One of the first mainstage productions at school was a lavish version of Sheridan's *The Rivals*. The entire school worked crew on this fantastic production, for which the ushers and the house was costumed and decorated for the period. They had harpsichord underscoring the entire play, and one of the juniors was in charge of music. So one night when I was on crew, I heard something intricate coming from the practice rooms upstairs and followed the sound, to a room where Steve was playing the piano and presumably writing the harpsichord parts. I said hello and asked if I could listen to him, and he explained musically what he was after; I was a director, as was he, but my mother is a classical pianist, and I earned college money working for the local symphony/opera company where I grew up in Syracuse. So that began a very long friendship, and I got to know him very well over the years. We both loved music and opera. And he had long blond hair and we were both very hippie-ish, even though we were serious students. Also, he was roommates with a boy I eventually dated, so we saw each other often and became even more special friends. And, *The Rivals* was a huge success. The funny part is, Steve can still play all the music from it." Upon graduation, Schwartz got a very impressive job right out of school, working as an executive in the artists-and-repertoire department at RCA, which gave him a solid career start and a leg-up in the recording business, but his more immediate dream was to see his lovingly-crafted *Pippin* emerge as a Broadway hit. Lansbury and Beruh absolutely believed that Schwartz was the new great hope in music and lyrics for theater, and that perhaps *Godspell* could, with hard work and some luck, allow him to create his initial stronghold as a powerhouse of the modern musical. Schwartz saw the show at LaMama, and immediately began revamping almost all of the compositions as well as the majority of the lyrics.

Thus, in a short amount of time and with very little discussion, Bolick's original score was out and Schwartz's new score was in. And initially, many involved weren't happy with this decision. "Quite candidly," said Peggy Gordon, "we really couldn't understand why our producers wanted to replace Duane's original music. It was melodic, and very much like what you would have heard on early-70s FM radio. But Edgar and Joe were in their forties, and it was a real generational shift for them to feel comfortable with music that, to them, sounded like rock & roll, as opposed to the kind of rock-theater music that had been popularized by *Hair*. They loved Steve's music when they heard him play his score for *Pippin*, so they felt his musical sensibility would be a better fit for a show that was breaking new ground as a theatrical hybrid: part clown show, part revue, part book musical. But poor Steve; we actually liked what we already knew of his music, but kind of displaced our anger toward our producers, whom we also grew to love, for dropping Duane's score. So, we reassembled after a few weeks off from LaMama. It was the night before our first rehearsal, on April 12, 1971. We were at Edgar Lansbury's house, and gave Steve a very cold reception when he played all the new music for us. But," she added, "I have to say how magnanimous he was to tell me that he tried to write something to replace 'By My Side,' but ultimately felt like, why do that when there was something already so perfect for that spot? Can you imagine someone choosing to share the spotlight like that, when he'd been given carte blanche to replace all the old music? So our resistance dissipated after the first few rehearsals, because Steve's vocal arrangements were so beautiful and just heaven to sing. As for the show itself, since we had five new songs (out of Biblical text and hymns) and one wholly re-conceived song, 'Turn Back, O Man' (which had been a gorgeous ballad and Robin's solo), we mostly integrated the new and then got to work either cutting or reshaping sections."

With the addition of Schwartz and his score, besides the additional input he gave to the direction of the show, also came Stephen Reinhardt as *Godspell*'s new musical director. "Up to the time I met Steve," Reinhardt said, "I had been a working professional dancer on Broadway, who happened to be a musician on the side. Steve and I met in 1970 after I spent some months writing songs. He was an A&R executive at RCA; I auditioned for him as a singer-songwriter, and we did some demos. Months went by, and then one day he called me and asked if I would work with him on *Pippin*, because he and I had similar playing styles. As I recall, we hadn't really done much, and then *Godspell* happened. We got together and he played the score, and handed me lead sheets. I think I recorded it also. I went home and started to learn it, mostly by ear. So there I was, suddenly a band leader in a musical, and I certainly wasn't nearly as good a pianist as I was a dancer. Though I had worked with many musical directors, I had no experience as a musical director myself. You must also understand," he continued, "that *Godspell* was like a magic trick that worked brilliantly no matter who performed it, but you didn't know why. I only knew *how* to do it. I was weaned on Rogers and Hammerstein, Bock and Harnick, and Kander and Ebb. Musicals like this weren't anything I'd ever experienced before."

Also with Schwartz came two changes in casting. Though all parties agreed that both Prudence Wright Holmes and Jimmy Canada were doing equally fine jobs in their roles, the composer wanted to bring two newcomers into the *Godspell* fold in their place. The first was Joanne Jonas, a recent graduate of the American Academy of Dramatic Arts who had worked with Schwartz in summer stock; her Bronx heritage in entertainment was huge as the granddaughter of theatrical agent Bert Jonas, besides being an accomplished triple threat in her own right as well as an inherent musician. The other was Lamar Alford, a loveable teddy bear of a man who hailed from an Atlanta suburb amidst a family steeped in the church; he possessed an enormous voice suited towards both gospel and opera besides flawless gifts for humor. Thus, with a brand-new and seemingly-perfect ensemble and all-new songs, besides an impending change of venue to the Cherry Lane, began the newest step in *Godspell*'s evolution.

Interestingly enough, the show also had no official choreographer. "What we had from that point on, and it was a blessing," said Peggy Gordon, "were both Joanne Jonas and Steve Reinhardt. Steve actually wore three hats; he was a musical director, a singer-pianist, and a dancer. Joanne and Steve were able to help us manifest dance and movement ideas into purposely-silly choreography. John-Michael wanted everything, every single element, to be in clown character, and that included the movement. Rather than slick, he wanted it to be goofy. And we all made some slight contributions to that besides what Joanne and Steve were coming up with. It was Sonia's idea, for example, that we do a faux-tap dance in 'All for the Best.' She talked about what children look like when they're learning to tap but haven't mastered the steps yet. It was a very funny illustration, and perfect clown behavior. And that's how all our choreography evolved for the most part." Stephen Reinhardt added, "The oddest thing I ever did in my life was to experience piecing *Godspell* together hour by hour. Or day by day, if you'll pardon the pun. It was a total group effort, a symbiosis. The sum was greater than the parts. Whatever talent we had, it was tapped. Everyone knew I had been a dancer, I knew all the stock soft-shoe steps, and so I trotted them out for Steve Nathan and David Haskell in 'All for the Best.' I knew the cake-walk, so we put that in the final chorus of 'Turn Back, O Man.' My gift, I suppose, was that I knew how to teach non-dancers this stuff, how to count it, how to get the feet on those counts. Later, in subsequent companies, I always taught the staging and dances."

Besides loaning her skills as a co-choreographer with Reinhardt, Jonas was also able to find a place in the company for the band she sang with on occasion. It starred her then-boyfriend, bassist Richard LaBonte, and his friends, guitarist Jesse Cutler and percussionist Ricky Shutter. Reinhardt recalled, "I didn't meet Richie, Jesse and

Rick until the first rehearsal. That's how it happened. We were these unlikely guys all thrown together, like a garage band who didn't know each other. But for whatever reason, and here's more of that *Godspell* magic, it worked perfectly." (It's interesting to note that later on, fans of the show worldwide would refer to the band as The Godspell Four). Further augmentations came to the music in the form of Alford playing the piano on "Learn Your Lessons Well," and for "By My Side," McCormick played guitar while Mylett provided accompaniment on both recorder and concertina. A final change very nearly took place involving Susan Tzu's costumes, which she took upon herself to rectify. "When it moved to New York, the producers bought the costumes from CMU for $150.00," she said. "Which was fine and fair, but all the interesting patches and appliques had been taken off. I reapplied them all myself, while sleeping at the Cherry Lane."

Opening night drew nearer and nearer; the final presentation prepared to open with the entire cast singing the nonsensical "Tower of Babel," Haskell and company on "Prepare Ye, The Way of the Lord," Nathan et al with "Save the People," and a standout moment for Lamont when she sang lead on "Day by Day" before being joined by all. Next was McCormick's high-spirited "Learn Your Lessons Well," and a show-stopping highlight for Jonas with "Bless the Lord" among the entire cast. Then came "All for the Best," sung by Nathan and Haskell, and "All Good Gifts," in which Alford would not only raise the roof but bring the house down. Closing the first act was "Light of the World," a rollicking group number with solos by Braha, Gordon, Mylett and Lamont, and intermission would be spent with the cast serving wine in paper cups to the audience before once more taking their places on the stage. Act Two also aimed to be a winner from the get-go; after a group reprise of "Learn Your Lessons Well," Manzano would slay the audience with "Turn Back, O Man," and in one of Nathan's definitive moments of the evening, he would then belt out the deep and intense "Alas For You," while hurling frustration at the Pharisees into all corners of the Cherry Lane. "By My Side" would showcase utter poignancy on the part of composer Gordon, and then would come the sprightly "We Beseech Thee," in which the throng could fall in love with Mylett. The action wound down with the ballad "On The Willows," before the climatic Betrayal by Judas and Jesus's Crucifixion on the chain-link fence, punctuated by Nathan and cast intoning, "Oh, God, I'm dying! Oh, God, he's dying!" and cutting him loose, parading him down the aisle on their shoulders in rigid cruciform to a reprise of "Prepare Ye." The show ended with another group rendition of "Day By Day," absolutely supercharged with energy. All would be interwoven with the carefully-selected parables that Tebelak had nurtured since that very first day back in college. The house was packed, the curtain went up, and *Godspell* was born.

As stated, the opening-night audience was completely electrified by what they saw and heard. The injured McCormick, who had to sit out the following two nights and was replaced by Faso, said, "I watched the show from the audience for the first time at that second performance, and I have to say I was practically dumbstruck. An actor's perspective is very limited on the stage, and I never really saw what my fellow actors were doing or how the whole piece moved and danced and exploded with such precision. You almost couldn't take it all in. Two sawhorses and three planks became a boat, or an altar, or a swing, or a table and any number of other things, and as an audience member you sometimes don't even see the change. That was the first time I was aware of 'what we had,' and I remember telling John-Michael that every single cast member should sit out one show and experience the piece as a whole. Which he thought was a good idea, but we had no understudies as of yet so it would have to wait. I was really proud of the show, and even more proud of its simple message of hope and peace, which was changing people's lives. It was theatre in its truest form." As an afterthought, Nina Faso added, "We had no understudies or standbys, so the cast carried me through the show on the second night while John-Michael threw up and shook with fear. He still had to call the show, and everyone was trying to do everyone else's job." She chuckled, "Thank God there are no pictures of that performance!"

Theater tradition of the day dictated recording an original cast album on the first Monday after opening night, and *Godspell* followed appropriate suit. Schwartz and Reinhardt painstakingly organized every detail, and the Godspell Four was never more ready (Ricky Shutter's percussion proved a particular standout, especially on the final refrains of "Save the People"). And most of the cast professed to have a wonderful time at the session. "The most remarkable thing about it to me," said Manzano, "is that we did the whole thing in one day," while Lamont added, "It was my first recording session ever! I had a ball, and fell in love with working in a studio. Although, I had some pitch issues with 'Day by Day,' but I think it sounds earnest enough." McCormick, however, didn't quite cherish the experience. "I have only a vague memory of that session," she said. "Not being what I call a singer, those sessions were probably very uncomfortable for me and I've simply blocked it out. All I remember is being very close together around a microphone, and the light wasn't very good." Gordon commented about not only the speed that it took but the length of time or lack thereof. "It was lightning fast, almost too fast. Steve Schwartz and I have commiserated about this, that we wished there were things we'd redone. But when you're in a hit show, and we were, the impetus to get the album out is great. We literally did all the vocals on our Monday day off, and it was a very long session. I remember glancing at the clock on the wall of the recording studio when it was time to record 'By My Side,' and it was something like 1:20 a.m. That's why I refer to it as my somnambulistic vocal!" Nonetheless, the album was pressed with the familiar logo on the front, featuring a Christ-like caricature by David Byrd in Art Deco shades of black, white and red, and a similar caricature of Stephen Nathan on the back in Superman jersey and makeup. It wasn't even the blink of an eye before the LP began to fly off of record-store shelves at an incredible rate. (Schwartz, as it happened, would later win two 1971 Grammy Awards for the album, one as composer and the other as producer).

Next, after a few months of playing to perpetually-packed houses, came the news that the first official out-of-town production of the show would launch at the Mark Taper Forum in Los Angeles. Flying out there would be David Haskell, Robin Lamont, Peggy Gordon, Lamar Alford, Jeffrey Mylett, and Herb Braha. Interestingly enough, Stephen Nathan just happened to be in Los Angeles at the time, shooting the role of the Courier in *1776* (in which he gave a very impressive performance on the song "Momma Look Sharp"), but a contractual obligation wouldn't allow him to make the nightly appearances as Jesus in *Godspell*, so Andy Rohrer joined his original CMU castmates to once again re-create the role. Rounding out the women were Jeannie Lange in the role created by Gilmer McCormick (Lange would become Haskell's real-life love-match and the two enjoyed a long and happy marriage), Rebecca Baum in the Sonia Manzano part, and a young lady from Joliet, Illinois by the name of Lynne Thigpen, who had somehow never done a professional musical before but perfectly embodied the role created by Joanne Jonas.

Thigpen, who post-*Godspell* enjoyed spectacular success not only on and off-Broadway but in film and television, always viewed the fact that she was "making it" in show business as a personal triumph for having been bullied daily as a child. "The kids at school used to gather around me every day," she once said, "and sing-song, 'Thigpen, Thigpen, lives in a pigpen.' Or they'd call me Lynne Pigpen or just Pigpen, probably from the Charlie Brown cartoons. I'd glare at them and clench my fists and say, 'One day I'm gonna be a big star and you'll all be sorry,' and run home while they all laughed. After *Godspell* came out, I was flown home to give a speech at my old grade school, and all of those big bullies showed up with their cameras and their autograph books so they could say hello to their 'good old friend Lynne.' They brought me in from the airport by limo, I walked into the school auditorium to thunderous applause, took my place at the podium and announced, 'I will only give my speech if the following persons are removed from the premises,' and I listed them all by name. They were all escorted out by school security and they couldn't believe I'd do that. And for the rest of my life, if I flew home to visit my family and I had to run to the store for a bottle of milk or something, any time any of them saw me on the street they'd cast their eyes to the ground and walk right past. If *Godspell* did nothing else for me, it was that."

Meanwhile, back in the Big Apple, Manzano and Jonas were joined by Elizabeth Lathram in Gordon's part, and another member of the Carnegie contingent, Katie Hanley, took over for Lamont. Jesus and Judas/John the Baptist were played by Ryan Hilliard and Michael Forella respectively, Howie Sponseller was in Braha's role (interestingly, Sponseller would soon go on to direct the Toronto company), Mark 'Binky' Planner took over for Alford, and a sensational young gentleman named Dean Pitchford played the Mylett character. Also, Randee Heller embodied the role

McCormick chose to vacate for the time being; she and Reinhardt had by this time also become a love-match (which continues to this day), and she wanted to travel to Boston with him to help oversee the musical aspects of the company there once the Los Angeles production got underway.

"It wasn't love at first sight," McCormick said, "but there was a definite attraction that wouldn't go away. I tried not giving into what I was feeling, because Stephen already had a beautiful girlfriend, and busting other people's relationships is not something I do. But as the days and weeks went on, I found myself falling hopelessly in love with him, and he with me. We were married between shows on February 12, 1972, and got that night off, for which Nina once again went on for me. No honeymoon, but a year later we went to Acapulco. I'm guessing we were already married when Steve went to Boston, but I'm not sure, because the only reason I didn't join the Los Angeles company was that I was cast as one of the leads in a movie called *Squares*, and I know we weren't married when I did that film. Honestly," she continued, "I wasn't sure I wanted to get married to anyone at all, but when Steve was sent to England to do the show there, I missed him so much that I realized quite clearly I wanted him in my life forever. Which was *the* best decision I ever made!" (As an aside, when the other original cast members were being transferred back to New York from California to resume their roles, Lansbury and Beruh moved the Taper company to a commercial theater, where the Robin Lamont role would be played by a young performer by the name of Judy Kaye, trained by Gordon to portray the part effectively).

Now a bonafide smash on both coasts and a true cultural phenomenon, as well as the fact that Schwartz received two Drama Desk Awards, companies of *Godspell* began sprouting throughout America and worldwide. The Boston company scored a huge hit, aided by CMU castmate Carla Meyer in the Peggy Gordon role, and a young man named Jerry Sroka in the Herb Braha part. The First National Tour was a complete sell-out, and featured in the role created by McCormick a young actress named Melanie Mayron, who would also play the role in the San Francisco company after the tour. And Toronto's original cast became one of the most legendary, featuring a group that included Eugene Levy (in Braha's role),

Andrea Martin (as the Jonas character) and Martin Short (playing Mylett's part), as well as a young lady from Detroit named Gilda Radner, who would embody the McCormick role. Jesus would be portrayed by a young theater performer and former folk-singing star named Victor Garber. And keyboardist for the company was an ambitious twenty-two-year-old by the name of Paul Shaffer, in his first professional job.

As if none of this was enough, "Day by Day" suddenly became a hit pop tune. Radio airplay was constant, and the song soared to Number Thirteen on Billboard's Top 100. Gordon recalled, "I stayed in Los Angeles for an extra two months after everybody went back to do the show in New York City, and I watched them all sing 'Day by Day' on the broadcast of the Grammy Awards. That was when I suddenly realized the scope of the show's immense popularity." "I wasn't surprised," Manzano added. "Most musicals only have one or two songs that transcend the show it's from, after all." Jonas said, "I think the first time I heard it was in an elevator," while McCormick chimed in, "My first time was probably in an elevator or grocery store, but I wasn't surprised that it became the hit of the show. Although I liked many of the other numbers a lot more, they were, nonetheless, 'show tunes' and were not, as they say, as hummable as 'Day by Day' certainly was. As a side note, shortly into our second run in New York, we read that 'the current Pope's daily prayer is 'Day by Day,' a well-recited prayer in the Catholic church.' That certainly didn't hurt the song's success." And Lamont, the voice behind the popularity of the song, never even heard it on the radio until 1972, when the alarm on her clock radio sounded for an early appointment. She said, "It was kind of surreal, to wake up and go, 'Is that me?' Honestly, though, I wasn't surprised that the song reached the top of the charts. It was always the one folks went home singing after the show, and of all the songs, can stand on its own the best, both lyrically and harmonically."

Angela Scott, who later became a notable comedian during the standup comedy boom of the late 1970s and early 80s, used to recall her own audition for the national tour. "I wasn't a singer," she said, "not at all. But I'd seen the show, and I thought it would be fun to do. So an audition was announced for one of the national tours, and I decided to go. When I walked in, they said, 'Can you sing?' I said, 'Oh, yes. Of course I can.' They said, 'Do you know "Day by Day?"' I said, "Oh, yes. Of course I do.' So the pianist started playing it, and I sang, 'Day by Day, Day by Day, Day by Day…by Day by Day…Day by Day by Day by, day-hey-hey, Day by Day by Day by, day-hey-hey, Day by Day by Day by Day by, Day by Day.' And I got the part. But they didn't have me sing 'Day by Day' in the show. Can you imagine?"

While all this was occurring, Lansbury and Beruh began entertaining the idea of "the little show that could" transferring onto the big screen as a movie musical. Response from the major studios, however, was tepid and half-hearted at first. Lansbury explained, "Once the play established itself, we talked about a film but without any specific goals. We were approached by independent companies and, I think, CBS, but we had no specific plans such as who would direct or how it would all take shape." But it was later in 1971, after the show's first London company opened at the Roundhouse Theater and then moved to the larger Wyndham (starring David Essex as Jesus and an unknown named Jeremy Irons as Judas/John the Baptist) that Columbia Pictures began to show serious interest. With producing partner Duncan helping to pull the proper strings and secure a production budget of $1.3 million, a deal was soon made to everyone's contentment, and the wheels were in motion to bring a celluloid version of *Godspell* to light, with pre-production officially beginning on May 14, 1972.

The initial question was whether or not Tebelak would also direct the film; even though the show was very much his baby, he had absolutely no experience with the movies. But the name that immediately sprung to Lansbury's mind to assume the directorial helm was that of David Greene. "David was a good friend," Lansbury said, "and a director I had worked with when I was an Art Director at CBS. We did many shows together at the beginning of our careers, including *Studio One, Climax,* and *Playhouse 90*. He was very inventive, and had a firm understanding of film technique and story. He was in London when *Godspell* moved on to the West End, so I invited him to see it and also suggested he come to Paris, to see the production at the Porte St. Martin, which we co-produced with Annie Fargue. He absolutely adored the show, and we discussed his directing the film. Of course, at this time, he met John-Michael

Tebelak and Stephen Schwartz, and I suggested to them that he would be a good choice to direct it. John Van Eyssen was our initial contact with Columbia; he was the Chief Production Executive for Columbia in the UK. John certainly knew of David's work, and felt comfortable with him, so we began to make plans."

David Greene was, in fact, already known to a small degree in New York and Hollywood, and much more so in the UK and Europe, as quite the colorful character and a true original. Born David Brian Lederman in Manchester and raised in Bethnal Green where his father owned and operated a barbershop, he also set his initial sights on a career as an actor as did Beruh in the 1940s, albeit in film and television. His on-screen debut took place in the 1948 British crime drama *Daughter of Darkness*, and then a more significant supporting role in *The Hideout* in 1949, alongside Valerie Hobson and Howard Keel (where a smaller supporting role was embodied by a young Michael Hordern). But after roles in such films as *The Golden Madonna* in 1949 opposite Michael Rennie, and 1950's *The Wooden Horse* in which he co-starred with David Tomlinson, he made his final on-screen appearance in 1951's *The Dark Light*. It was here that he would also meet and fall in love with fellow trouper Kathleen Blake, who became the second of his seven wives (his first marriage, to Margaret Lane, ended in divorce in 1948 after seven years). Fancying a much more lucrative career behind the camera than in front, he directed several episodes of *Hallmark Hall of Fame* in 1951 shortly before his final dramatic appearance in an episode of *Goodyear Playhouse*, and throughout the 1950s and 60s spent most of his time working in television either as a writer, director or producer or combination thereof. Greene's big-screen directorial debut came with the horror film *The Shuttered Room* in 1967, starring Gig Young, Carol Lynley and Oliver Reed, and then the 1968 romance flick *Sebastian* with Dirk Bogarde and Susannah York, but he worked in television in between, directing several episodes of *Coronet Blue*, produced by Lansbury. 1970's *The People Next Door*, with Eli Wallach and Julie Harris heading up an equally-stellar supporting cast, was his most critically-acclaimed effort to date, and Lansbury was therefore certain that Greene was the ideal director to bring *Godspell* to life.

Once Greene was firmly locked in, Lansbury's next move was to enlist Kenneth Utt as associate producer, with whom he'd worked most notably in a similar capacity on *The Subject Was Roses*. "I liked Kenny enormously, we became good friends when we first worked together on *The Defenders*, and he was indispensible on *Roses*. And since *Godspell* became a 'New York film,' he was the right man for the job," Lansbury said. Now a team was truly being assembled, with Greene and Utt calling most of the shots as far as hiring. Brian Eatwell had worked as production designer on two other Greene films, 1968's *The Strange Affair* and *I Start Counting* in 1969, and was an ideal choice. Another excellent recruit was cinematographer Richard Heimann, who had made a great career in television commercials. Lansbury recalled, "He was young, hungry, and extremely resourceful." One of Utt's largest contributions was bringing in editor Alan Heim, with whom he'd worked on the award-winning television special *Liza with a Z*, starring Liza Minnelli and directed by Bob Fosse. "I was not a fan of *Godspell*, being nonreligious," Heim said, "and everything I heard about it really made it seem slightly sappy. But Kenny offered me the job, and I met with Greene, who seemed to want a commercial editor who could do 'flashy' editing. I suggested that if David shot 'flashy' material, I would give him a 'flashy' cut. And that seemed to sell him."

Godspell's original costume designer from day one, Susan Tzu, was never actually asked to take part when pre-production began. Her initial concepts would be used in the film, particularly the now-trademark Superman jersey with suspenders and rainbow-striped slacks for Jesus, but designer Sherrie Sucher made some slight modifications to the wardrobe here and there. Sucher, who at age twenty-three was the youngest costume designer ever invited to join United Scenic Artists, was very much a specialist in the 'Objets Trouvés' style that was already such a requisite element of *Godspell*'s presentation, and here again Lansbury felt that her involvement was absolutely inspired. Art director Ben Kazaszkow was part of Lansbury's intrepid team from *Coronet Blue*, and John Godfrey had served as set decorator for *The Subject Was Roses*, where production manager Paul Ganapoler had also been assistant director.

One key element was the hiring of an actual choreographer for the film where there hadn't been one for the original stage show, and the logical choice was Sammy Bayes, who had drawn tremendous acclaim for his direction and staging of the show's first production in Australia shortly before. Bayes had started out as a Broadway hoofer and protégé of Jerome Robbins, serving as dance captain for *Fiddler on the Roof* and ultimately assistant choreographer for the film version, and also choreographed the short-lived musical version of *The Canterbury Tales* for Broadway in 1969, for which he received a Tony nomination. He recalled, "I'm not even really sure how it happened with *Godspell*, but they sent for me and I met with David Greene. We hit it off, and I got the job. And I didn't really give a lot of thought to the outcome, just that it was going to be an exciting and enjoyable challenge." Joanne Jonas would assist Bayes on the film, just as Nina Faso would assist the producers. Three final major players who were hired included Phil Goldblatt and Phylliss Sagnelli, for makeup and hair respectively, and television veteran Belle Halpern was engaged as script supervisor.

Of all the original creative team behind *Godspell*, it was Stephen Schwartz who had the most trepidations. "I remember being surprised that a film version was being contemplated so soon," he said, "and I worried that the release of the movie would shorten the run of the show, as those were the days when a movie tended to hurt a show's business as opposed to boosting it. On the other hand," he added, "I worried unnecessarily." A concern that loomed larger was exactly where Tebelak would figure in, as Greene wasted very little time in establishing his territorial rights to all possible areas of the movie. Among other things, he decided to take Tebelak's initial theatrical vision of an empty world and convert it, cinematically, to a world empty of people. He also demanded to be credited for co-authoring the screenplay, although Tebelak retained additional credits for originating the book for the stage and as creative consultant for the film. This caused a small degree of animosity between the two both professionally and personally although not, as was rumored later, a fur-flying knock-down drag-out war. (Greene would later add salt to Tebelak's wounds when, after being questioned by journalists about the controversy, he sent a letter to *Variety* which said, in part, "Tebelak and I are enjoying an ideally-smooth working relationship. But he is not co-directing the film with me. He did not write the screenplay. He participated only minimally in pre-production planning and discussions, and attended very few rehearsals." To which Tebelak told a friend, "I guess Greene was directing a different picture then, since I was there every day for every phase of every element before, during and after. Or maybe he was just every shade of ridiculous. Let's go with that one.")

Eventually, there arose the biggest hurdle of all, namely the casting of the film. Historically, original casts from the theater didn't normally re-create their roles on screen. Even such stars as Mary Martin and Ethel Merman were almost never cinematically cast in the parts they'd made famous on Broadway; notable examples of these include the fact that Julie Andrews played Maria in *The Sound of Music*, Mitzi Gaynor portrayed Nellie Forbush in *South Pacific*, Deborah Kerr was Anna in *The King and I*, Betty Hutton embodied Ms. Oakley in *Annie Get Your Gun*, and Rosalind Russell sallied forth as Mamma Rose in *Gypsy*. Conversely, Barbra Streisand played the title role in *Hello, Dolly!* instead of Carol Channing, Natalie Wood was Maria in *West Side Story* after the stage portrayal by Carol Lawrence and, in what was one of Hollywood's most unusual choices, the aforementioned Ms. Andrews was passed over for Eliza Doolittle (the role she created both on Broadway and in London) in *My Fair Lady* in favor of Audrey Hepburn (with Marni Nixon providing the vocals, as well as those of Misses Kerr and Wood in the previously-mentioned pictures). What chance, then, did a relatively-unknown ten-member ensemble, even from one of the biggest musical hits in modern theater history, have of being cast in the film? It had been whispered, and then established, among the *Godspell* company that a movie version was very much in the works, but none of the actors had a remote clue as to whether they'd also get the opportunity to play their roles under Greene and the lens. Jeffrey Mylett, in his typical fun-loving and curmudgeonly fashion, devised a game backstage (the show had by this point moved from the Cherry Lane to the larger Promenade Theater), where all had to decide which popular stars of the day would be playing each of them in the film (one notably-amusing idea was that Carol Burnett would embody the Gilmer McCormick role and that Rita Moreno would go on for Sonia Manzano).

"I don't think anyone knew who would be part of the film cast," said Robin Lamont. "Rumors floated for awhile as I recall, and the original cast was, in no way, a shoo-in for the movie. I believe there was also talk about casting one or two celebrities, although I don't know who in particular or how serious it was. Suffice to say, none of us 'actors' were privy to what the Columbia executives were thinking, and if Edgar and Joe knew, they certainly weren't saying. The process was quite competitive, and went on for at least a couple of months." However, even though it turned out that Lansbury and Beruh leaned very heavily towards casting all of the members of the original Off-Broadway company, and Schwartz and Tebelak hoped that would be the case, the final decisions were left to Greene as to how the scenario would play out.

Greene did feel that nobody besides David Haskell could possibly bring Judas/John the Baptist to life more effectively, although if another could possibly be found, using that gentleman's talents in the role wouldn't be ruled out completely. He felt likewise about Jeffrey Mylett, Peggy Gordon, Sonia Manzano, and Gilmer McCormick. The rest, however, remained a large question mark. It was at this time, with the approval of Columbia Pictures as well as Lansbury and Beruh, that Greene decided he would merely travel to all of the companies of *Godspell* currently playing worldwide and make his casting decisions through process of elimination, beginning with a careful new look at the company in New York. Upon seeing both Robin Lamont in the role she created and then Katie Hanley in the same part, his immediate impulse was to cast Hanley. But in this instance, Tebelak resolutely put his foot down and was supported wholeheartedly by Schwartz. "Day by Day" had become an enormous hit, they reasoned, and Lamont's voice and charisma were largely the impetus behind the song selling a million copies; would Greene honestly want to risk not employing such a winning combination in the film? He concurred, and was eventually very pleased with the choice of keeping Lamont in the role, but hoped he would find a way to somehow utilize Hanley's beauty and impeccable talents if at all possible. Greene also absolutely adored Joanne Jonas, and insisted that she be retained as Bayes' assistant on choreography, but he was completely electrified by Lynne Thigpen in Jonas's role when he traveled out West to scope out the talent among the Los Angeles cast, and decided she simply must play the part in the film and sing "Bless The Lord" in the movie. As such, he couldn't for the moment imagine how to also incorporate Jonas, the actress who had created the part, onto the screen, especially in light of the fact that she'd obviously be on the set every day.

As it happened, he didn't have to worry. Sonia Manzano would be absolutely unavailable; she had just gotten cast in a brand-new TV show called *Sesame Street*, produced by the Children's Television Workshop, a forum not only for Jim Henson's Muppets and to teach very small children the fundamentals of reading and arithmetic, but the chance for her to be the first Hispanic leading lady on a mainstream series, in the role of Maria. Contractual obligations and time constraints, therefore, would completely prohibit her from doing the role or "Turn Back, O Man" at all whatsoever, either on stage or screen. Then, fate frowned upon Peggy Gordon. "I got a wicked case of tonsillitis that took me out of the show in early June, and also out of the movie," she said. "When Gilmer and Steve Reinhardt went to Toronto to work with the company there, I house-sat for their cats, Sam and Charlie. Gilly had this big bag of brownies in the apartment when I got there, and I threw them in the garbage for fear I would eat them, only to fish them out after the show later that night. And I ate every single one. I woke up the next morning in terrible pain, could barely swallow, and thought it was due to the brownies. Edgar Lansbury immediately got me in to see this ear-nose-and-throat specialist named Dr. Gould; he examined me, picked up the phone, called Edgar, and said, 'She's out of the show temporarily, and out of the movie completely.' After I cried and whispered 'Why?' he explained that this was the worst case of tonsillitis he'd ever seen, and that he couldn't operate until I was completely free of infection. That took the entire month of June, and the operation was in July. Recuperation took a month, and then by August I could sing again, but it was too late for me to be in the film as an on-screen character because they'd begun working two weeks earlier." It was at this point that Greene decided that Katie Hanley would play Peggy Gordon's role, splitting some of the action with McCormick, while Jonas and Thigpen would take on different areas of both Jonas's original role and Manzano's, featuring Jonas singing "Turn Back, O Man" and Thigpen's mighty delivery of "Bless The Lord."

Hanley said, "The first time I heard about a film being done of *Godspell*, I was in the dressing room at the Promenade. A few of the cast members were whispering about it, saying that Sonia wouldn't be able to take part because she was committed to *Sesame Street*. Then someone, I truly can't remember which girl, said that I was being considered. It left me in a bit of a daze as I thought about how the show would translate to film, and I think it was too large for me to grasp. One thing was certain; we weren't merely a cast in a production. There was a uniquely bonding '*Godspell*ian' spirit among the cast, and the thought of anyone being excluded felt both odd and sad. In any case, I imagine that my agent confirmed that I was cast in the film, and I do recall feeling elated and honored. I clearly remember how gracious Peggy Gordon was when she phoned to congratulate me, and her kindness was evidence of the root system of the show she took part in creating.

"I have to laugh when I think about walking over to Bloomingdale's, after I knew I would be doing my first film," she continued, "and trying to open a charge account. I was denied because of my profession. Before the salesperson approached me, I'd already picked out my first couch, a bed with a real headboard, and a dining room set. I was certain that I would no longer have concerns about money for the rest of my life; I was in a movie! That's truly the logic of a naive twenty-three-year-old. The anticipation of such huge fulfillment was at the forefront, so credit card rejection was incidental. But also," she said, "I didn't expect to become famous, nor did I anticipate that kind of change in my cast member's lives. My goal was to become a Broadway actress, and that had happened twice before I ever did the film. I was living in the midst of my dream, and simply couldn't conceive of anything on a bigger scale than all that I was already living; it was impossible to broaden my horizons any larger for myself or my castmates."

With the women's roles firmly settled, it was time to give thought to the gentlemen of the ensemble besides Haskell and Mylett, who, by now, Greene felt would be impossible to replace. (This was testament to each one's talent indeed, since Jeremy Irons was very much in the running to play Judas/John the Baptist, and likewise Martin Short for his handling of Mylett's character in the

Toronto production). Herb Braha, though quite imposing, happened to be very light on his feet, a top-notch master of movement and also gymnastics; his cartwheels during the show were always a standout, and he also possessed tremendous comic ability as well as marvelous aptitude for mimicry and character dialects. Greene, however, wanted someone in the role that wouldn't quite dwarf the screen in the same way, and it was after he saw the Boston company that he knew Jerry Sroka would be the perfect choice. "The show in Boston was a huge hit," Sroka said. "I mean, huge. Lunch with the Mayor huge. Dinner with Henry Cabot Lodge huge. Want to shoot a commercial? Done. Huge. So huge that the restaurant next door to the Wilbur Theatre, The Beef and Ale, not only held a table for us nightly, but sent free beer. I mean, free beer? C'mon! We were making three hundred bucks a week, every week, which I figured was more money then anyone would ever need. I was meeting girls in the laundromat and they were putting quarters in my machines. It was that kind of huge. So when word came, I think it was in our seventh or eighth month, that there was going to be a film, we were all pretty damned excited. Although, it was with the knowledge that the original cast would probably be in the movie and not any of us. After all, they had percentages. Then rumors started that David Cassidy would play Jesus, and then a rumor that Columbia Pictures would see every company before making any decisions on casting. Bingo. We had what we thought was the best company; why would we be any different than any other company? We weren't given any warning as to when David Greene would visit, we only heard afterwards. And of course we were trying to remember if the show went well that night. Several weeks later, I got a call from the Lansbury/Beruh office saying that I had been cast. I also got a call from Herb Braha, who congratulated me and wished me well. I'll never forget that. You must also understand," he continued, "that the first time I saw *Godspell* on stage, I had just been cast. I had two dollars to my name and it was a job, an actual job in the theater; I was happy to be working. I saw the show the day after I got cast, and I was blown away. I laughed, I cried, I had never been so moved. My best friend, Lloyd Bremseth, was our Judas/John, and we live ten minutes from each other in Los Angeles. We never tire of reliving our ten months in Boston or our eventual time doing the show together in New

York. The Boston company was the first company to play in a large house, twelve hundred seats. And the producers were worried the show wouldn't fly; the Cherry Lane had a tiny capacity, and the Promenade was three hundred seats, so nobody knew if the show would work in a large house. But did it? Like magic. Standing ovations every night. So I knew it would work, at least I felt it would work, on film, having conquered both large and small houses. Doing the show was a gift, but getting the film was an even bigger one. I couldn't wait to begin and create new moments that would live on. I knew that Greene had seen me in the show, so I felt that I knew what he wanted. He had a wonderful laugh, where his head would rear back, and from his gut a loud full English roar would emerge. So I knew I had something. He was in my corner from the first day; I had dinner at his apartment in New York several times, and we became good friends."

Then there was the question of Lamar Alford. He was, of course, also a bulkier fellow, and in physical possession of a head that at times and from certain angles appeared oversized for his body; it was completely uncertain how he might look under the scrutiny of the camera. In turn, Greene in his travels found absolutely no one, in any company of the show, who could remotely hold a candle to Alford's celestial rendering of "All Good Gifts." The only talent search employed by the film (other than Greene's forays around the globe to scout the other companies) was dispatched, and young Merrell Jackson from Chicago was discovered, primarily a dancer but also an extremely promising comic actor and a more-than-capable vocalist, even though neither his physical characteristics nor his singing voice remotely resembled that of Alford. "Merrell Jackson was chosen for his youthful looks and his voice," said Lansbury, "which had a quality that was particularly appropriate for the harmonies in the score." Although later, when recording for the soundtrack album got underway, there was talk of the top notes on "All Good Gifts," which for Alford's heavenly operatic belt had been a walk in the park and not so for Jackson, being more effectively showcased if overdubbed by Ben Vereen or a similar performer. Nonetheless, Schwartz and Reinhardt would slightly modify the vocal arrangement to accommodate Jackson's impressive falsetto. (Alford, it turned out, was utterly unconcerned with whether or not he'd be in the film. One day when his close friend, the playwright Robert Patrick, was visiting him, he pulled open a desk drawer to look for draft of a script he'd been writing, and it was bulging with checks in many sizes and colors, a good deal of which spilled onto the floor. "Oh, that's just *Godspell* money," he said to Patrick by way of explanation. "They send those things to me faster than I can cash them. Pay no attention, please.")

Now came the final and arguably most important decision to be made; who exactly would be playing Jesus in the film? It was all but a foregone conclusion that it wouldn't be Stephen Nathan; he was still very busy with *1776* and other professional commitments in Los Angeles, although he remained one of both Lansbury and Greene's primary choices. Clearly, it had to be someone who possessed both the talent for the role and truly-extraordinary looks, and at one point rumors were circulated that Jesus might be played by any number of current teen idols, however unfounded. In fact, Greene's personal first choice was David Essex, who had played the part so marvelously in London opposite Jeremy Irons and budding British stars Gay Soper, Julie Covington and Marti Webb. Essex had the physical height required to make Jesus truly electric on the screen, besides dashing good looks and exquisite vocal abilities. But if Greene had any pre-conceived notions about who should play the part in the film, these were immediately discarded when he made his final casting stop in Toronto and saw Victor Garber play the role for the first time.

Garber and his two siblings grew up in London, Ontario; his mother was at one time the popular Canadian band singer Hope Wolf, and she later also became a television actress. Young Victor's own star quality and talents for entertainment were undeniable by the time he was nine, as evidenced when he was accepted into the Children's Program of the Grand Theater, and at age sixteen attended a summer program at the University of Toronto. But his first true success came not as a theater performer but a folk singer, when he founded the quartet The Sugar Shoppe at age eighteen, and the group experienced success with their recordings as well as appearances on American television, presented by Johnny Carson and Ed Sullivan among others. He proved a natural to play Jesus in *Godspell*'s Toronto company, and only learned secondhand that he'd been cast in the film. "I read it in the newspaper, soon after we'd opened our production at the Royal Alexandria," Garber said. "Greene was seeing all the productions currently playing in different parts of the world looking for a cast for the film, and we were the last company he saw. The next thing I knew, in an interview, he said he had found the Jesus for the movie and that it would be me. I found the whole idea rather odd, to be honest. I was still quite young, I'd never made a film, and much more daunting was the notion that I'd be playing Jesus among a cast of people I'd never met before, some of whom had already known each other and worked together in the show. But whatever misgivings I had were soon dispelled, once I met everybody."

Indeed, an entertainment workplace is very similar to any other job environment, or even the first day attending a new school, especially when being thrown into a concentrated group of people who've known each other before and not only established a rapport, but already knew what would be expected of their efforts. In the case of *Godspell*'s cast, a mercy was that this would be a major motion picture debut for all. But some friendships already existed among them; Lamont, Haskell, McCormick, Hanley and Mylett had known each other since college, and they'd already worked with Jonas as well as Thigpen. McCormick and Thigpen had also already established best-friendship, and Thigpen and Jonas were equally close. And Jonas had known Sroka from a previous show they'd done together. But Garber and Jackson were complete newcomers to the group. However, even those who'd been part of the *Godspell* family from the very first became ultimately enthusiastic, albeit in varying degrees, to welcome new friends into the flock. McCormick said, "I best recall that it was from a fellow cast member that I first received the news that I was cast in the film. More in my memory, though, were my feelings when I heard the news of who *wasn't* cast. Unreasonable or not, there was a feeling of ownership in *Godspell*. It was a highly-successful product of our combined imaginations and talents, and it just didn't seem right, or logical for that matter, to tamper with that approach while moving into the next step. It was sad, and got even sadder when we heard that our parts were going to be mixed up. My feeling was that I had created the Gilmer character, and I wanted to play her, not bits and pieces of others. I was afraid the balance would be lost. But," she continued, "my feelings about 'the substitutes' had nothing to do with the feeling that there never should have been 'substitutes' in the first place. Victor, Merrell, Lynne, Katie and Jerry were/are all fantastic performers in their own right, and each had done the show on stage with other companies. I grew to love everybody, and Lynne and I truly became best friends if we weren't already. It's just that I would have liked to play the big game with my own team, as it were."

Jonas said, "It felt very different to be doing a mash-up of me, the Joanne role I'd created for the stage, and Sonia's part. And honestly, Greene had at one earlier point said to me that he loved what I did in the show, and later said that they were in a pickle because Sonia couldn't do the movie. They had this wild idea that perhaps I could do her song and wear her costume, and have Lynne sing my song and wear my costume, but I'd mostly keep the parts that I did in the show. I did lots of funny voices, and they really liked that, because I was almost like the female counterpart of Jerry. And Lynne and I were such extremely close friends that it was wonderful to share all that with her. My feeling was, 'Hey, ya know, I love *Godspell* and I'm not attached to what I do in it. Lynne is one of my best friends, and she will sing the daylights out of 'Bless The Lord,' plus I'd love to sing 'Turn Back, O Man.' I remember thinking, or maybe even saying, 'This movie will never be like the show, and so I'm just going to enjoy the flex and shift in making it.' Besides, it was my first film, and beggars can't be choosers. As for the newer people, I'd say I got along with everybody. Victor seemed a bit soft to me at first, but he was so pretty and also so talented that I could understand why they wanted him. Merrell, too. He was very sweet. I never really got to know Katie as closely, but I found her a very interesting person and actress, and I'd say we got on very well."

Hanley's experience was quite different from the others. "I didn't feel that I had the right to take issue with any of the casting for the film; I was just grateful to have been chosen. When I met Victor for the first time, he talked a lot about the cast in Canada, and I didn't feel part of that. I was accustomed to feeling part of my *Godspell* folks. I'd known many of them at Carnegie-Mellon, even if I wasn't in the show way back when it started at school. So it was foreign to hear stories from our new 'leader,' our new Jesus, about people like Gilda Radner who were, at the time, unfamiliar to me. It felt disloyal to my 'clown,' as illogical as that may sound. I wanted our Jesus to be ours, without mention of any others. But," she added, "I'd worked with so many gifted stage actors whose talents awed me, and when I met Victor Garber, I knew I was in the presence of a great star. I have to also say, I felt sad that Lamar wouldn't be doing the show, and Merrell was so soft-spoken and gentle, just so much Lamar's opposite. But we all grew to love him, because he was just so sweet and so dedicated."

"I had taken a break from the show, and was on vacation when I got the word from my agent that I had been cast," said Lamont. "I didn't find out who else would be in it until I returned to New York. And I was extremely happy. It's every young actor's dream to be in a film, and being in *Godspell* meant that in any part you played, you had a major role. I'm sure I thought the film would be a natural stepping-stone to a more lucrative acting career, especially in film. For the most part, I was just happy to have been chosen. We all knew the casting was highly competitive, after all. So I was delighted with the final results. I had worked with Lynne and knew she was a great choice, and of course I knew Katie, and her infectious personality that always came across on stage. I knew that Jerry Sroka was a standout in the Boston production besides other shows he had done. And I'd never seen Victor perform the show, but when I first met him I got it right away. I sensed his charisma, I heard his singing, and it was obvious why he was chosen. To be honest, Merrell was the only cast member about whom I had reservations, because of his shyness. But it wasn't long before he fit right in. He had an incredibly warm, expressive voice, and was a total sweetheart of a guy. The bottom line is, there were many, many actors, some that I worked with and some that I didn't, who could have done equally well in our roles. Luck and timing had a great deal to do with the casting, like it usually does."

From the start of the summer of 1972 for nearly the next two months, *Godspell* was thrown into a whirlwind of plans. Of course there were costumes to be fitted, and Hanley had an interesting recollection of the event. "Before filming, I met with David and the costume designer, Sherrie Sucher, about what I envisioned. Since each clown is based upon the essence of who we are, I was asked about a costume that I felt summed me up best. I thought about how I wore my hair in kindergarten, pulled up tightly to one side with a ribbon, saddle shoes with white socks, and then described my high school days as a cheerleader for the football team. Shortly after this meeting, I was asked to come to the 'fashion show' for David at the Cherry Lane Theatre, where we'd all walk onto the stage and show him what Sherrie had come up with for my costume. She showed me some jeans she had worked on tirelessly, with patches carefully sewn on to cover every square inch of them. They looked amazing, but when I tried them on they turned out to be hip-huggers, and the shirt and small vest I was to wear were very short, so my entire midriff was exposed. I was horrified, and refused to come out of the dressing room. David put up with my shyness, and asked Sherrie to come up with something else. She must have been pretty ticked off, because she came up with a skirt that came from the bottom half of a formal gown or something. It was poufy, it fell to the middle of my calves, and was very unflattering. To make it worse, she gave me green bloomers to wear under the skirt, with a big football jersey covering my waist, a vest to cover that, and a boa covering my neck. I felt like a pumpkin. I told Sherrie that the skirt was too long, and took a big safety pin and pulled one side of the skirt up so I could move a little better. The pin stayed in as part of the costume in the movie. We probably should have gone with the patchwork jeans, huh?"

There were also locations around New York to be scouted and shooting permissions granted by the Mayor's Office of Film, additional crew to be hired, initial publicity to be launched, and each member of the cast had to join the Screen Actors Guild if they weren't already members. Not to mention those who were still appearing in the stage productions at the Promenade or elsewhere, who had to continue fulfilling their obligations. And as with any film musical, the very final step of the pre-production process towards unleashing *Godspell* onto the screen was by recording the soundtrack of the score.

A&R Studios in New York was engaged for the sessions on a two-week series of scorching-hot days in late July, as opposed to simply one Monday in between shows, or with just a small band of four musicians. This time around, Reinhardt would serve as associate musical supervisor, and once again the original Godspell Four would be front and center to provide the musical base. "I knew Steve liked the way we played the show," Reinhardt said, "and in the beginning there was a slight sense of getting whoever we could to be involved. By the time the movie was in pre-production, he could have had anyone he wanted for the recording, but he liked our feel, the way we played the score." But Steve Manes would be on hand for every session as an additional bassist and Don Thomas would play guitar, and aside from the fact that Schwartz himself would once again also provide his own inimitable styling on keyboards, he would be aided by Paul Shaffer, the young man from Canada whose first professional job was with the Toronto company. Reinhardt said, "Paul was to our show what Billy Preston was to the Beatles. Just flat-out genius at his craft. I ran across him while up in Toronto, when he was the pianist for the final auditions, and he just blew me away, so I suggested to Steve to bring him to New York to play on the film. That's how he arrived in the United States, and how he got his start here."

Above and beyond all of this, and to give the music a much more well-rounded sound apropos to a film soundtrack, six string musicians (including such major sessions players as Elliot Rosoff and Norman Carr) and three trombonists (among them Mickey Gravine) also played on every number, and George Devins provided percussive accompaniment on timpani when needed. Individual instrumentalists were engaged for specific songs, among them Michael Kamen on synthesizers for "Alas For You," Charles Macey to play banjo on "All for the Best," and for "Prepare Ye," Chayim Tamar would blow the ceremonial Shofar horn. Also on that track, as well as "Day by Day," was solo lead guitar by Hugh McCracken, arguably the greatest session player of the time as well as now, and who had already recorded with nearly every major musician and vocalist of the day. Reinhardt recalled, "Hugh's solo style was very blues-based, and 'Day by Day,' being pop, it required more of a George Harrison-type approach. Which wasn't the way he played, so it took him a while to figure out. It ended up being absolutely brilliant, but I think it still wound up a little more bluesy than Steve might have preferred."

Recording "Day by Day" would also prove a far more satisfactory experience for Robin Lamont this time around. She said, "We weren't rushing through it, we didn't have to get home to rest up to go on stage the next night. And we had all of the extra accompaniment, plus the majority of us had had studio experience at that point. I had no pitch problems this time around, and it's absolutely the recording I prefer of the two." Unfortunately, the rest of the cast encountered a difficulty they'd equally suffered the first time, namely the handclaps involved to help bring the rhythm to life. "Our poor cast," said Schwartz, "had to do the clapping in 'Day by Day' until their hands hurt, just as they had had to for the original cast album." "It *was* pretty awful for them," Reinhardt agreed. "These were the claps done over the end credits and extended 'Day by Day' sequence. The claps went on forever, and then had to be doubled. At one point, everyone was thinking about the pain more than accuracy, so we had to do some pick-ups to clean them up. It was brutal. I think even I was out there clapping along." Hanley recalled, "I vaguely remember the 'clapping session' in the studio for 'Day By Day.' A bit hard on the hands, but in retrospect it was nothing compared to writhing on the cyclone fence at the end of the show or the film; I clearly remember getting blood blisters and was appalled. But, as far as clapping for Stephen Schwartz? I would have jumped through hoops for days for him if I'd had to." Lamont said, "I do remember that we had to do the clapping over and over. Can't recall why, but it was just that if you didn't clap in a certain way, doing it all together it didn't sound like clapping. It was just a weird noise. I think we had to keep our hands in a slightly open position to get a bit of the hollow sound, and of course, we all had to clap on the beat. I could be wrong, but maybe toward the end, Steve Schwartz just had a few of us clapping and they doubled that track. If he did in fact do that, I wouldn't have been one of the few who were clapping; my sense of keeping time is not as strong as some of my other creative qualities."

Executing the remainder of the recording was by and large a proverbial piece of cake for all concerned. "Of course we had the addition of some orchestral 'sweetening,' and the amazing Paul Shaffer on keyboards," Schwartz said, "and I had an excellent engineer in Eliot Scheiner. But basically I went about doing it the same way as

I did the original cast album, in terms of how it was tracked, etc." "We had been playing the show for a year, after all," said Reinhardt, "so we knew it cold. But recording is so very different from playing live. When playing live, you're in the moment with the band, with the cast and with the audience. In the studio, you're listening acutely. You're aware of every note. You're aware of 'you.' It's fun and exciting, but it's also nerve-wracking. You don't want to screw up, even though anything can be fixed." He also contended that the easiest track of all to record from his own perspective was "By My Side," for his only having to play on the last fifteen bars.

Two other musical elements wouldn't prove quite so simple, for Reinhardt or otherwise. First, the songs "Learn Your Lessons Well" and "We Beseech Thee" had been cut from the movie, thereby disallowing both McCormick and Mylett the solo numbers they'd gotten to enjoy night after night in live performance. Both would still enjoy short solo sequences in "Light of the World," and McCormick, as always a self-professed non-singer, was somewhat relieved by the prospect even if it meant less time on camera and further diminished the role she'd created. It clearly must have been a different situation for Mylett, a truly riveting and accomplished vocalist, for whom "We Beseech Thee" had always been a highlight of the second act and a spectacular display of his talents. "I felt very badly about that for Jeff," Reinhardt said. "He and I had become close friends." Whatever Mylett's reaction at the time isn't known or readily remembered, but it couldn't have been easy for him to then learn that both songs would be used as instrumental underscoring, in the pivotal 'Prodigal Son' sequence that takes place at none other than the Cherry Lane. In any case, this particular section of the score is an uptempo, almost honky-tonk, rendering of the two which, while appearing on the screen to be played by Garber as Jesus at the piano, was in fact recorded using two pianos; on one, Schwartz would play with both hands while Shaffer played the other with just his right. Whatever anyone's hurt feelings over the inclusion of either song or lack thereof, the end result remains a feat of superb musicianship and technical wizardry.

The second came in the form of "Beautiful City," the only new song Schwartz wrote for the score. "Steve felt he needed a new hit song for the movie," Reinhardt said, "but it was tough for me, at the very least, because it felt like it was still warm in my hands when we had to work with it." However, the song, with its inclusion of lush refrains by harpist Corky Hale as well as a 'bubblegum-style' melody and outlook of lyrics became, if nothing else, a cult favorite among *Godspell*'s legion of worldwide fans when the soundtrack became available for commercial release; it might well have gone on to be as big a hit as "Day by Day" if recorded by the right singer or band of the time. Reinhardt said. "I remember when Steve first played it for me; I just watched that right hand keep going and going on those triplets, and I could see it easily as a hit. 'Raindrops Keep Falling on My Head' had been huge only a year before, and it had that same flamboyant, carefree whimsy." "I was very excited about 'Beautiful City,' but recording the soundtrack was the most fun for me anyway," Garber said. "I was used to singing in a studio, and I felt comfortable there. And Stephen was so sure of what he wanted, and so smart." Sroka added, "I actually got to hear it before we went into the studio. I had a meeting with Edgar Lansbury and Joe Beruh at their office, and Joe told me to say hello to Stephen Schwartz, who was down the hall. I knocked and walked into an office the size of a postage stamp, a two-cent postage stamp at that. It was just Steve and a piano. He looked up, we hugged, he sat down and asked, 'What do you think of this?' And he played and sang 'Beautiful City.' I told him it was not only perfect, but beautiful, which I guess was appropriate. And," he finished, "I not only love that sequence in the film, but it's probably my favorite song." Schwartz himself, who has expressed sincere joy at the fact that the song has had a renaissance since the events of 9/11 in New York, never gave any thought to whether or not it would have gone on to greater glory. "I think if the movie had been a larger commercial success in its initial release, perhaps 'Beautiful City' might also have been a bigger hit. With the benefit of hindsight now, of course, I'm not sorry it wasn't, because I find the original lyrics fairly simplistic and naive, and I far prefer the rewritten version that I did several years later for a benefit concert following the LA riots. Now, the revised version is used in most productions of the show, and I feel it is greatly superior, both lyrically and musically, to the original version I wrote for the movie."

Finally, after exactly three months to the day, pre-production was complete. Every song on the soundtrack recorded, every stitch sewn, every line learned, every design designed, and every speck of ink on the contracts was dry. And at the center of it all was a grinning and self-satisfied David Greene, who surely retired to bed on August 13, the night before shooting began, secure in the knowledge that he was about to re-invent the modern movie musical.

Unfortunately, hundreds of others involved in the company went to sleep that night feeling not quite as confident. But either way, all were braced for the first new step of the journey. Day would come soon enough, and with it, hopefully, the light of the world.

PHOTO GALLERY

First costume test, full cast, Carnegie-Mellon, 1969. (From l.) Martha Jacobs, Sonia Manzano, Randy Danson, Robin Lamont, Jamie Stevens, Mary Mazziotti, Andy Rohrer, Stan King, David Haskell, Bob Ari.
PHOTO COURTESY SUSAN TZU.

First costume test, full cast, Carnegie-Mellon, 1969. Andy Rohrer and company.
PHOTO COURTESY SUSAN TZU.

First costume test, Carnegie-Mellon, 1969. Randy Danson.
PHOTO COURTESY SUSAN TZU.

First costume test, Carnegie-Mellon, 1969. Jamie Stevens.
PHOTO COURTESY SUSAN TZU.

First costume test, Carnegie-Mellon, 1969. David Haskell.
PHOTO COURTESY SUSAN TZU.

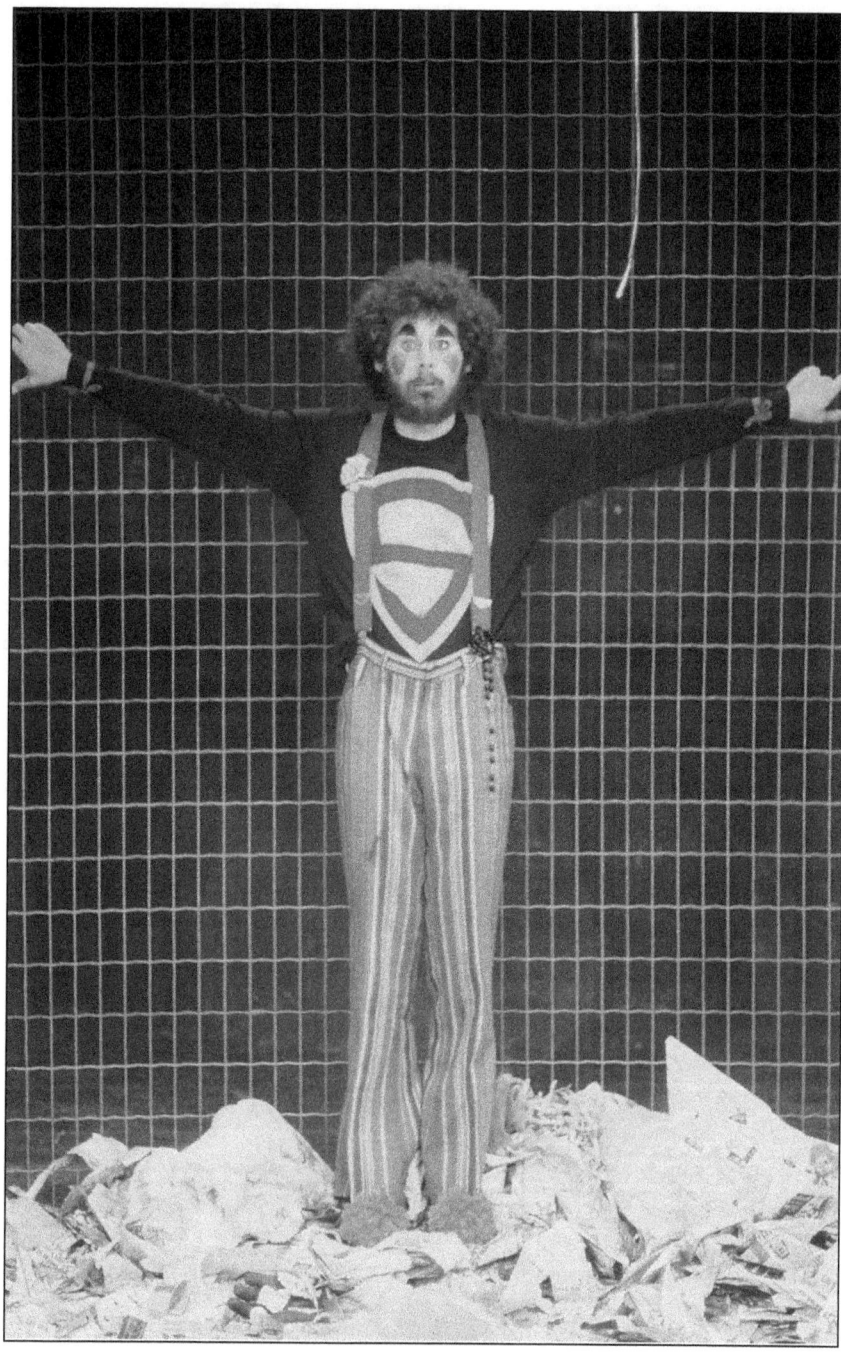

First costume test, Carnegie-Mellon, 1969. Andy Rohrer.
PHOTO COURTESY SUSAN TZU.

First costume test, Carnegie-Mellon, 1969. Sonia Manzano.
PHOTO COURTESY SUSAN TZU.

First costume test, Carnegie-Mellon, 1969. Martha Jacobs.
PHOTO COURTESY SUSAN TZU.

First costume test, Carnegie-Mellon, 1969. Bob Ari.
PHOTO COURTESY SUSAN TZU.

First costume test, Carnegie-Mellon, 1969. Robin Lamont.
PHOTO COURTESY SUSAN TZU.

First costume test, Carnegie-Mellon, 1969. Stan King.
PHOTO COURTESY SUSAN TZU.

First costume test, Carnegie-Mellon, 1969. Mary Mazziotti.
PHOTO COURTESY SUSAN TZU.

The David Frost Show, 1971. Second Off-Broadway company singing "Day by Day," led by Katie Hanley. (from l.) Michael Forella, Mark 'Binky' Planner, Howie Sponseller, Elizabeth Lathram, Sonia Manzano, Dean Pitchford, Randee Heller, Joanne Jonas.
PHOTO COURTESY KATIE HANLEY.

The David Frost Show, 1971. Second Off-Broadway company singing "Bless the Lord." Ryan Hilliard, left. Front row (from l.) Katie Hanley, Sonia Manzano, Randee Heller. Middle row (from l.) Elizabeth Lathram, Howie Sponseller, Joanne Jonas. Back row (from l.) Michael Forella, Mark 'Binky' Planner, Dean Pitchford.
PHOTO COURTESY KATIE HANLEY.

Backstage visit with Helen Hayes, Promenade Theater, 1971. (From left) Michael Forella, Dean Pitchford, Katie Hanley, Sonia Manzano. PHOTO COURTESY KATIE HANLEY.

Girls' dressing room, Promenade Theater, 1971. Katie Hanley, front. (From l.) Elizabeth Lathram, Sonia Manzano, Joanne Jonas.
PHOTO COURTESY KATIE HANLEY.

Director David Greene (behind camera) with cinematographer Richard Heimann and crew, 1972, setting up a shot on Broadway and West 52nd Street.
PHOTO COURTESY ROBIN LAMONT.

Cinematographer Richard Heimann (left) prepares Victor Garber for a close-up, Ward's Island, 1972.
PHOTO COURTESY KATIE HANLEY.

Creator John-Michael Tebelak reads the Times during a lunch break on Ward's Island, 1972, while Jerry Sroka (right) enjoys a good book.
PHOTO COURTESY KATIE HANLEY.

Script supervisor Belle Halpern, Ward's Island, 1972.
PHOTO COURTESY KATIE HANLEY.

David Haskell between takes, Central Park, 1972.
PHOTO COURTESY KATIE HANLEY.

Gilmer McCormick relaxes between takes in Central Park, 1972, while Lynne Thigpen (left) catches a nap.
PHOTO COURTESY KATIE HANLEY.

Jeffrey Mylett between takes, Central Park, 1972.
PHOTO COURTESY KATIE HANLEY.

While setting up for "Day by Day," Robin Lamont enjoys a quick coffee, Ward's Island, 1972.
PHOTO COURTESY KATIE HANLEY.

In between takes on the tugboat for "Light of the World," East River, 1972. (From l.) Lynne Thigpen, Gilmer McCormick, Joanne Jonas, Katie Hanley, David Haskell, Victor Garber.
PHOTO COURTESY KATIE HANLEY.

A makeup-free moment at Grant's Tomb with (from l.) Katie Hanley, Robin Lamont and Jeffrey Mylett, 1972.
PHOTO COURTESY KATIE HANLEY.

Rehearsing 'Parable of the Good Samaritan,' Ward's Island, 1972.
Gilmer McCormick, Jerry Sroka, Katie Hanley.
PHOTO COURTESY KATIE HANLEY.

Dance rehearsal, Part One, "All for the Best," full cast, Lincoln Center, 1972.
PHOTO COURTESY KATIE HANLEY.

Photo Gallery

Baptism take two, Bethesda Fountain, 1972. (From l.) Jeffrey Mylett, David Haskell, Katie Hanley, Lynne Thigpen, Robin Lamont, Joanne Jonas.
PHOTO COURTESY KATIE HANLEY.

Rehearsing 'Seed Parable,' full cast, Ward's Island, 1972.
PHOTO COURTESY KATIE HANLEY.

Robin Lamont waits for the cameras to roll on "Day by Day," Ward's Island, 1972.
PHOTO COURTESY ROBIN LAMONT.

A moment of surprise for Lynne Thigpen and Katie Hanley, Lincoln Center, 1972.
PHOTO COURTESY KATIE HANLEY.

David Haskell and Victor Garber rehearse shooting their silhouette for "All for the Best," 1972.
PHOTO COURTESY KATIE HANLEY.

Rehearsing the defeat of the Pharisee Monster, full cast (minus Gilmer McCormick), Chelsea Piers, 1972.
PHOTO COURTESY KATIE HANLEY.

Full cast, exterior of World Trade Center, 1972.
Photo courtesy Katie Hanley.

Lynne Thigpen and Gilmer McCormick at *Godspell* premiere, Lincoln Center Film Festival, March 20, 1973.
Photo courtesy Gilmer McCormick.

Victor Garber, Robin Lamont and David Haskell arrive at DeGaulle Airport, Paris, for 1973 Cannes Film Festival.
PHOTO COURTESY ROBIN LAMONT.

Cast, creator, director and producer, Ward's Island, 1972. Front row (from l.) John-Michael Tebelak, David Greene, Edgar Lansbury, Katie Hanley, Lynne Thigpen. Middle row (from l.) Merrell Jackson, Joanne Jonas, Jerry Sroka, Victor Garber. Back row (from l.) David Haskell, Gilmer McCormick, Robin Lamont, Jeffrey Mylett.
PHOTO COURTESY ROBIN LAMONT.

Part Two: Day by Day

In ninety-nine out of every one hundred cases, the art of filmmaking is a completely non-sequential process. What we as an audience see from the first scene to the last is almost never in the order that the action is filmed; different scenes are shot in different locales and then ultimately edited together piecemeal for the sake of cohesion. *Godspell* would be that rare one-hundredth case, because David Greene chose to shoot nearly all of it in precise script sequence, but for some locations for which Columbia Pictures was still waiting to secure permits. In light of the fact that different portions of New York would be the easel upon which the cast and crew would ultimately paint the picture (pardon the pun), it made perfect sense in the long run.

The stage show opens with the Prologue, in which the cast (minus Jesus and John the Baptist) are more or less shown going about their daily lives and dressed in somber clothing, muted shades of black, white, gray and light blue. Upon hearing the triumphant call of the ceremonial Shofar, they are born again and baptized in order to "Prepare Ye, the Way of the Lord," and after Jesus appears to John in bathing trunks for his own baptism and intones the mighty "Save the People," the cast are now sprung forth as true Disciples, dressed in every color of the rainbow with a variety of ornamentation, and all join in on the last chorus. Greene's vision for the big screen wasn't dissimilar, but now we would first truly see each of the eight members living their humdrum existence in their jobs and day-to-day affairs, albeit with a certain dimension to their character; Mylett would be a taxi driver whose way to alleviate stress in bumper-to-bumper gridlock was by tootling on a recorder, Jackson a garment center worker wheeling a rack full of dresses while bopping along to the music from his transistor radio, and Thigpen as a college student obsessed with a library Xerox machine, among others. The action would open with Haskell as John, a fully-loaded cart in tow, cheerfully making his way across the Brooklyn Bridge into Manhattan, then cut to each of the cast in different locales going about their business until, confronted with visions of John along with the pervasive sound of the Shofar, they are drawn to Bethesda Fountain on Central Park South to sing "Prepare Ye, The Way of the Lord" and join in their communal baptism in the water.

Katie Hanley would be playing a waitress at the Empire Diner, trying and failing to read her copy of James Joyce's *Ulysses* while customers loudly clamor for coffee. "The first day of shooting for me began with the waitress scene, at that diner in the city that was in an actual silver trailer. It was probably well-known by New Yorkers at the time, but I didn't know anything about it at all. I remember that I got to my first day of filming, we rehearsed it a little bit, and then they said that the make-up artist wouldn't be there and I would be filming without make-up. I was a little disappointed, but it was my first day in a feature film, and that was foremost in my mind, to put it mildly." She continued, "David Greene told me that he decided I should be a waitress, because he was certain that I would be the worst waitress in the world. He put a book in my hand, *Ulysses*, which I considered a compliment, and I became an easily-distracted waitress. Without make-up, and with way too many freckles." It's interesting to note that Stephen Schwartz made an uncredited cameo appearance in that scene, being served a cup of coffee.

Robin Lamont's character was that of an anonymous woman window-shopping at FAO Schwarz on Fifth Avenue and 58th Street. "I was simply given a call time and location of where I was to be, which was a trailer parked somewhere on Fifth Avenue. And I remember onlookers watching me go in and out of the trailer wondering who I was, and figuring I must be someone they should know. It was a daytime shoot, and I probably took the subway or a cab to get there. We shot my part right there, smack dab in the middle of Manhattan at FAO Schwarz, after a little bit of rehearsal. Between the crowds watching, the newness of the cameras, lights, film crew, etc, I was pretty nervous. Although, soon enough, there wouldn't be time to get nervous about anything."

"I was flown in do the first day of shooting in Central Park," said Jerry Sroka. "What we all found out much later was that it was also a sort of screen test, for Columbia to okay us. I'm glad we didn't know. We rehearsed on whatever was the locale for the day and shot. We all knew our clowns, so it wasn't astrophysics or anything. But the rehearsal for the new dances were excruciating for me. I was always a beat late. You know, Sammy Bayes had a full head of hair before he met me. The other thing about that day was that it started the tradition of Victor Garber and I having breakfast-eating contests. The breakfasts on the set from Craft Services were pretty damn good, and we filled our plate or plates more than once until one of us gave in. Those overalls of mine hid many, many pancakes." "Yes, the first day in Central Park was really the screen test," Hanley agreed. "We had to get on our costumes and simply talk a bit, say a few lines, etc., while the camera was going. There was some buzz between cast members that David Greene wanted to see how we looked on film, and a rumor that if there was something that displeased him, we might be replaced. After the screen test was viewed, David took me aside and told me two things. First, that he had gone to all of the different productions of *Godspell* across the country, and had handpicked his favorite actors for the film. He told me that there was a quality of reverence that he saw in me when I sang to Jesus, and he was very kind in all that he said about my talent and presence. Secondly, he said that he saw 'concern' in my face, and wanted to soften it with a red hat. 'When the concern lifts, dear Katie, I will simply yell out during filming, OFF WITH THE HAT!' Within a short time, he yelled it out on the set; I threw the hat back onto my shoulders for the rest of the film, and we moved on.

Of course Joanne Jonas was wearing two distinct hats of her own, one as co-star and the other as assistant choreographer. "I vaguely remember getting to a bus or motor home, which housed our dressing rooms, etc. The first they shot of me was the scene in the ballet studio with my partner, which actually took place in two locations, one at Showcase Studios and the other at Broadway Arts. Where, for the record, I had auditioned for *Hair* at an earlier time and got cast, but my mother wouldn't let me be in a Broadway show where I had to be naked. Anyway, David and I had to dance ballet. I had a lot of fun in the moment with my dance partner Daniel Levins, an amazing danseur, but then Haskell was to 'pop in' like he was doing with everyone in the Prologue. So Sammy got creative, and decided to do it while I was being lifted. David was not a dancer, and didn't know the first thing about how to do a ballet lift, from behind yet, so one of the grips had to hold my lower legs while David appeared to be holding me on the down side of the lift, dance with me a bit more, and then lift me again while holding my legs, switch partners and have Danny be back. It took a long time. My armpits hurt, and we laughed so much. And then it really paid off on film after editing. I think it was one of the more challenging openers which introduced the players to the on-screen action." She continued, "Assisting Sammy was a whole other matter. He and I would work out new stuff at the locations beforehand, and then I'd rehearse the parts with the other actors on the morning of the shoot, while the set was being dressed or the cameras being set for the shots. There was tons of waiting, so we always seemed to have plenty of time."

"What I loved most," said choreographer Sammy Bayes, "was honestly every single aspect. When you choreograph for a movie, the first creative period is the time where ideas germinate, as to approaching the staging of a musical number or scene. First I was given the conceptual approach to the piece by David Greene, then invited into the creative circle of everyone else seeking to fulfill that concept. I spent a lot of that time pitching ideas back and forth on approaching the presentation of a number. And the even more exciting part of my earliest time on the film was scouting the right locations, parts of the city that wouldn't just visually best serve our ideas, but even at times affect a change in our concept of a particular number. So going from all that into the actual shooting was amazing, because now I'd be working with the individuals, the actors, whose talents and personalities would help me to make all the pre-production ideas a reality."

After the individual pre-Baptism scenes were completed, with and without Haskell's appearances therein, the fun really began to creep back into *Godspell*'s spirit with the shooting at Bethesda Fountain, impossible to truly rehearse but nonetheless a party unto itself. "David Greene asked us who'd like to be the one to jump in headfirst," Hanley said, "and I offered to do it. He asked if I was sure I could do it in one take, and I said I would. It was fun going for it, and it really was done in one take. But that water was COLD!" "There was quite a bit of pressure to get it right," said Lamont, "since it involved everyone getting soaking wet. We all had a change or two of costume, but re-shooting the scene from the top meant getting the girls' hair dry, re-applying makeup, and change of clothes, and not for just one character, but for all. Once you did that, the light changed, and a new set up was required. But it felt good to be back together again as a cast. And from then on, we were together almost all the time as a group." McCormick agreed, "One of my favorite scenes was the Baptism at Bethesda Fountain in Central Park. I thought the scene was beautifully shot and edited. And soon after that, of course, was 'Save the People,' which was amazing. The quick, quiet close-ups between Jesus and John the Baptist amid all the splashing and color and music were particularly effective, I thought. I think all the cinematography in general, in the first scenes, was wonderful."

Also, this was the first time a scene was shot without anyone besides the cast being shown on camera, bringing Greene's vision of a world devoid of people to life. "It did seem odd when New York 'emptied' on any number of days during filming," McCormick said. "I remember looking up and down and all around, there wasn't another soul to be seen outside the ten of us. Of course I knew that behind every doorway and window, and around every corner, there were thousands waiting for the 'road block' to lift, allowing them to get on with their lives, but at that moment it was more like being in a sci-fi movie. It was eerie." "I wouldn't say that having the streets empty felt odd," said Hanley, "at least not for me. I was in the midst of something that felt so enormous, and can still to this day hardly believe I experienced. It was thrilling! At that moment, our movie felt like such a big deal, so big that the city itself had to bow down and be quiet." "It only looked empty," said Jonas. "There were lots of onlookers behind barricades watching us." "The operative word here is not 'odd' with regard to that," said Bayes. "At times it was challenging to design staging that worked with both David Greene and Richard Heimann to accomplish the look of an empty city, but very seldom did that fall on me personally. Those two gentlemen really did their homework in that regard, and things went very smoothly." Lamont said, "It didn't feel odd to me, because we didn't view the dailies to actually see what New York looked like 'empty.' For us, there were always people around. Most times, onlookers were polite and respectful. New Yorkers are used to seeing movies being shot in their city, and they'll stop and take a look, but then move on. Occasionally, we did have some police presence, just to set up barriers and remind folks to stand back. It was harder, I think, to act with the notion that New York was *quiet*. No people, no noise. Unfortunately, not so. We stopped filming more often because a fire engine was going by, or there was a subway screech beneath a sewer grate, or because of general city traffic. Of course, our speaking parts were overdubbed later, but sometimes the noise in the city made it hard to hear the music or directions that Sammy or David might be giving while a scene was in progress."

"The entire film had been shot MOS," said Edgar Lansbury, "so in post-production we had to dub all the dialogue besides lay in the music tracks, under the supervision of our dubbing editor, Jack Fitzstephens." MOS is a standard abbreviation in the language of filmmaking; its technical translation is "Motor-Only Shot," although a more commonly accepted definition is "Mit Out Sound," which has been alternately credited as first being used by Ernst Lubitsch, Fritz Lang, and Erich von Stroheim. Others define it as "Motion On Screen." However it was defined here, it boggles the mind to realize that all of *Godspell*, from the first frame to the last, shows not one syllable of dialogue as it was spoken on the set in front of the lens. "I didn't even remember that we had to do all of the looping later," said Sroka. "I certainly recall that we all wore microphones. But I guess we must have had to overdub everything, because there was always certainly a lot of background noise. One ambulance a block away could ruin a perfect take, and always right at the very end of the scene. I don't even remember New York being empty, except for the problems the assistants had with crowd control, but while we were shooting, the fact the city was empty never dawned on me. We were very focused." But Hanley vividly remembered the looping. "During the overdubbing session, I clearly remember being struck how quickly and successfully we all caught onto how to do it. I'm pretty sure that none of us had overdubbed a film before, and yet, it made sense that the same timing was required in singing together, as well as the improvisations we were called upon to pull out of our hats on the set. When I did the film *Xanadu* many years later, I had to go in for a few overdubbing sessions, and it came back very quickly. I'd say that's proof that learning in a positive and safe environment is the best! And, I can't even begin to describe how powerful it was, during the overdubbing, to see the film in black and white. As we watched the film, without the grand distraction of color, I remember feeling once removed from the film, and transformed from actor to audience member. That overdubbing session was the most intimate memory I have with the cast." "I have a better memory of looping the dialogue than I do of recording the soundtrack," Jonas said. "That was so odd, and to watch it, knowing it was changed later, was even more so. Like, the voice for 'hard as a rock' was supposed to be a la Mae West, and they thought it was too suggestive. Instead, they had me do this silly chippie-type of voice, which makes me wince whenever I hear it."

Naturally, aside from cast and crew on location, it was also a full first day for editor Alan Heim as the initial dailies began to filter in. Greene, Bayes, Schwartz and Kenneth Utt were always present while Heim worked his own brand of wizardry. "I just wanted to make a good picture and have fun while doing it," Heim said, "which has been my rule for my whole career, with greater or lesser success. Let's not forget, I was a very unlikely candidate for this project because I wasn't that big a fan of the show or the music. When they offered me the job, I went to the Promenade with David to see the play. This was when he was still deciding who would and wouldn't be in it, from all the different casts around the world. Unfortunately, because David was in the audience, the cast was playing right to him; after all, they wanted to be in the film and they knew he was there. That was disconcerting, and in general I thought the show was too broad and not something I wanted to do. Kenny Utt suggested I go back and see it again incognito, so I did, and I found the magic in the show. From that moment on, I was completely on board. And I have absolutely not one negative thing to say about the experience or anyone involved. The cast and crew were a delight, especially David and Sammy Bayes. I remember the cameraman, Richard Heimann, was very worried about his future career, because most of what he'd done up until then was commercials and he was nervous about it. Stephen Schwartz was a bit aloof, but a real pro, even then. And it was a pleasure talking to the cast members, because they seemed eager to absorb everything."

In addition to all the other business of the first day, cast and crew learned that they would have an unexpected and heartily-welcome daily visitor, namely David Greene's six-year-old son Nicolas, commonly called Nic then as now. A product of Greene's third marriage, to Eileen Grace Jack (which ended in divorce in 1970), he was on vacation and fully prepared to enjoy himself. "I went with my father to see *Godspell* on stage in London," he said. "David Essex was playing Jesus, and David really liked him and wanted to cast him for the film. Obviously that didn't happen, and Victor Garber ended up with the lead. I remember asking David about that, and he said it hadn't worked out with David Essex, but that the guy who was going to do it was really good and he really liked him. I guess I was excited about him doing *Godspell* because I could relate to it as a kid; the music was great and it was an engaging production. To be honest, I was not that involved with the whys-and-wherefores of David's career. He worked solidly from the 1950s to the 90s, so it was more a matter of 'this is what I'm doing next' and my going out to the States to spend the summer. But I will say that being on the set of this movie was magic. I was five or six at the time, so we're talking fun from a kid's point of view. Because I was the director's son everyone was nice to me, but I didn't think about it in those terms at the time, of course. It was just this cool place with lots of nice people, who were pleased to keep me entertained whilst Dad worked. I couldn't really name a favorite scene to watch being shot, because I was busy playing. I doubt I watched more than one or two takes; at that age doing anything more than once was painfully boring. But the cast were all lovely people. I don't want to upset anyone if I don't remember their name clearly, but I particularly recall Jerry being very funny and a lot of fun. And I remember playing a lot with Gilmer. She was like an older sister, I guess (not having had one), and we'd play with her tiger puppet that she carried in the movie. And we'd play the recorder. Oh, and I remember Jeff, who wore a bowler hat with a raccoon tail. I think, because this was not your typical 'Hollywood film,' that there was an absence of 'I am so interesting' amongst the cast. They were kids who suddenly were in a real feature film and they were having a blast. Honestly, I can't say I have any bad memories of it at all. I think the only thing that puzzled me was that when shooting finished, we no longer hung out any more."

Another regular portion of the daily routine was when Greene would call the final "Cut!" and everyone could go back to being themselves. Hanley said, "I took a cab to the first day of shooting, and I'm sure I either took a cab home, or walked. That was the nice thing about being young, unspoiled, and living in New York. The city was exciting enough, as was being a working actress, surrounded by so much talent. The height of luxury was going to a deli and meeting up with everyone else after work, never running out of things to talk about, and caring passionately about each other." Lamont agreed, "We'd usually stop filming when the light started to fade, or change to the degree that it wouldn't match the beginning of the scene. It was during the summer for the most part, so we had light until 7:30 or so. Afterwards, many of us would go grab a bite to eat, and then go home and rest up for the next day."

With the Prologue, Baptism, "Prepare Ye" and "Save the People" officially in the can, the next phase involved the initial locations on Ward's Island, shooting "Day by Day." Lamont explained, "Often, we needed to adjust the choreography once we were on the set, depending on the location. This was particularly true when, unlike the stage version, we had to travel from one place to another, i.e. up a hill in Central Park or the stone staircase, or following Jesus down the road at Ward's Island. We did spend quite a bit of time improvising for 'Day by Day,' since it took place at the 'playground' in Ward's Island, which wasn't completed until our first day of shooting there and we didn't have the set pieces to work with. It's during 'Day by Day' that the playground gets transformed from its dull, inhospitable space to one that has been 'touched' by Jesus and his new Disciples, and becomes colorful and full of fun. We would play around with the set pieces and props while the crew set up cameras and lighting, and talk about the ideas with John-Michael, Stephen and David. I imagine the woman who provided continuity, I'm sorry if I can't remember her name, was very busy for those few days, since the set decorators had to re-paint the set according to our improvised 'bits.' I'm equally sure that John Godfrey and his crew were *not* happy about that. Also, when we shot on Ward's Island, we took a bus, usually leaving from Central Park West in the 80s. It was always anxiety-provoking to think you might miss the bus, because in the movie world, that's a serious infraction. Katie had the most difficulty in getting there on time, and we were always waiting that extra five minutes for her. But she had a little daughter, and getting child care at that hour wasn't easy. I have fond memories of watching for her out the bus window, saving a seat, and having her plop herself breathlessly next to me just before the bus took off. Those were days when no one had cell phones to call in and say, 'I'm on my way!'"

Hanley had much more to worry about than missing the bus or "Day by Day," however, as the unit repaired to Fordham University's Lincoln Center campus for what would be one of her pivotal scenes. "The 'Seed Parable,' which we shot just after 'Day by Day,' was very hard for me," she said. "Since I hadn't been part of creating this particular clown character, and was only familiar with doing a rather brash, tomboyish 'Day By Day' Robin-type clown onstage, I remember feeling a bit lost when I had to deliver the lines I'd seen Peggy do in a gentler way. As the camera started rolling I had to just wing it, but I didn't yet have much of an identity in the film that was comfortable for me. I felt disconnected, and a bit lost. And, in that one-hundred-degree weather plus the hot lights, they had to keep putting cold towels around our necks. Anyhow, as we filmed the group scenes, I would stay in the back of the pack. One day, David Greene pulled me aside and said that he was noticing that I was in the back too much, and asked what would make me comfortable. I'm not sure what my answer was, but I know that the conversation ended in David asking me if I could roller skate. I told him that I hadn't since childhood. He laughed, told someone to get me roller skates, and burst out with more laughter, 'There, now you'll have a reason to be in the back!' It proved to be a blast! And it was *hysterical* when I heard them adding the roller skate noises to the film during the looping sessions. Especially at the beginning few measures of 'All for the Best' a little later on."

"Turn Back, O Man" would be shot very shortly thereafter inside Carnegie Mansion (the family estate had graciously given the company shooting rights on the property, so proud and proprietary had they felt about the show being borne at Carnegie-Mellon) with its priceless antiques draped with cloth, and this was obviously the favorite moment for Joanne Jonas as well as Sammy Bayes. McCormick also recalled it fondly. "I thought the filming in Carnegie Mansion was one of the best photographed and imagined scenes in the movie. And I have a memory of seeing Joanne's wig for the first time and couldn't imagine why she was wearing it." Robin Lamont felt otherwise, saying, "Up to that point, we'd shot everything outdoors, so it was extremely confining." Stephen Schwartz also said, "I felt that 'Turn Back, O Man' lacked a strong cinematic concept." But all involved had more than plenty to say about the shooting of "All for the Best," one of the only sections of the film shot out of sequence from the others, which came next and took nearly a week to complete.

A sort of three-act musical unto itself, the first portions feature the cast frolicking about Lincoln Center's exteriors led by Garber as Jesus, then Haskell as Judas singing his solo from a raft in a rooftop pool, a cigar in hand. This went off with nary a problem, as expected; Bayes's choreographic concept was reasonably simple and didn't much differentiate from the way the number had been played on stage. "My way of thinking," he said, "is, if it's not broken, don't fix it. When something works, use it. I like to use what the actor has to offer. If they're comfortable with the movement you give them, they will give back with their performance. So I tended, and still tend, to 'assist' by shaping and accessorizing movement natural to their bodies." It was also the section of the film where Hanley arguably never looked quite so beautiful, when she close-danced with Garber and gazed into his angelic visage.

The second portion features Jesus and Judas atop the Bulova-Accutron sign in Times Square, doing their counterpoint duet and soft-shoe routine with canes, while an oversized silhouette of themselves dances on the big screen behind them. "That was technically a challenge," said Edgar Lansbury, "coordinating the dancing with a pre-shot screen." For editor Alan Heim, however, it was a cinch. "We programmed the sign, and I was up in the control room behind it. Over a shoe store, as I recall. They just did the same dance in front of the lights. I really love that montage; it's one of my favorite parts of the entire movie."

The third and final portion featured the entire cast dancing atop the then-unfinished south tower of the World Trade Center. Of course, audiences today across the globe, and particularly in New York City, experience a swell of emotions when seeing the Twin Towers in all their historic and spectacular majesty on the screen, as does the cast and everyone else who was involved in the film. But more than this came momentary terror for some and utter exhilaration for others, and sometimes a mixture of both. "It's the most difficult part of the movie for me to watch," said Sroka. McCormick said, "We were up so early that morning, way before dawn, and we were told to report to the crew elevator at ground level. It was dark, and cold, and we were all so tired. Adding to that, I had a terrible fear of heights. Knowing we'd be dancing on the roof of the then-tallest building in the world did not help alleviate the growing anxiety in my heart. Lynne, who was of course my best friend, thought it nothing but a great adventure. So together, we stepped into this tiny elevator and began our ascent. Which took forever! When the door finally did open, there we were, standing on what was then the top floor, the open windows billowing wildly with plastic, lights and wires and cameras and makeup tables and all sorts of movie stuff and staff milling about all over the place, all in semi-dark. You could feel the tower swaying in the wind, and even though we were assured many times that this is exactly what it was supposed to do, I personally felt little comfort. Soon, I knew, I was going to have to climb that steel ladder up to the roof, and my anxiety increased with each moment. When places was finally called," she continued, "it was Lynne who helped me, or I should say, actually pushed me, up onto that ladder and out onto the roof. The sun was just coming up over the East River, and turning in any direction, you could truly see forever. The sheer beauty of the panorama was so awesome that I slowly forgot my fear, and I followed Lynne ever closer to the edge, but safely so. The wind was fiercer the closer we got, and then suddenly Lynne stopped and began to spread her arms way up and out, in a sort of flying gesture. Pretty soon I was doing the same thing, and there the two of us stood for probably only a moment or two, but it seemed like ages, arms outstretched, leaning our bodies into the wind, riding it like a surfboard, feeling the soaring power that a bird must feel when it flies." She finished, with a touch of melancholy, "When all those people fell from those towers on that dreadful morning in 2001, I immediately thought back to that day, standing with Lynne on top of one of those towers. And, perhaps in an effort to replace a horrifying thought with a comforting one, I liked to think that only their bodies fell to Earth; their spirits lifted into the wind, and with arms outstretched, soared like birds to heaven."

"My least favorite scene to shoot, by far, was the dance number atop the World Trade Center," Lamont said. "It was open, but I'm afraid of heights, and simply being up that high made me nauseous with anxiety. Worse, we had to do some of the number at the *edge* of the Trade Center, with our backs to the perimeter. You couldn't see where you were going. The building wasn't completely finished indoors, so we'd take the elevator to the top floor and then have to walk a few flights, and finally climb a ladder to the opening at the top. It was quite unpleasant. And Jeffrey didn't help, because he would make as if to jump off, thinking this was quite funny. I didn't." "The most awesome to shoot, for me," said Jonas, "was on top of the World Trade Center. The helicopters shooting us, the building wasn't finished, and it was both scary and thrilling. The choreography aspect of 'All for the Best,' however, was something of a nightmare, and not just the scene on top of the Towers. It's really one of the only scenes in the movie that's shot in a lot of different locations all over town, both on top of the buildings and the Accutron sign plus the portions near Lincoln Center, and it literally took days before it was finished and we could move on." "What I remember," added Hanley, "was walking up many flights of stairs, with freezing-cold winds blowing through the steel beams at the top of the building, and that was one of the proudest memories of my life. We were to shoot from the top of this unfinished masterpiece, in the second tower, early in the morning. This kind of filming, from a helicopter above us was, I believe, a first at that time. To have been in the building as it was being built, looking through the beams out to the city, and to have been so close to something in history that our country will never forget, is an honor to have as a memory. Also, it was so cold, walking up all those stairs to the top of the second tower, that the crew had placed small hibachi ovens, one on each side of each step, to keep us warm enough." Editor Alan Heim said, "I particularly liked the ending shot on the top of the still-unfinished tower, with the frightening helicopter shot as the tag. The pilot didn't want to get too close to the structure, because he had no idea of the effect of the building wall on the rotors." Stephen Schwartz summed up, "My favorite sequence was 'All for the Best,' because I thought it was the most imaginative use of empty New York. I enjoyed being there for some of the shooting of that number, including the scary and exhilarating day on top of the unfinished World Trade Center, swaying alarmingly in the wind."

Once solidly returned to the comfort of terra firma, it was time to shoot the "Parable of the Good Samaritan" at Ward's Island. What followed was the 'Parable of the Sheep' at Grant's Tomb, which went off without a hitch for the most part. Jonas said, "It was the first time I had been to Grant's Tomb. You know you live here, as a native New Yorker, but sometimes never get to experience it. I do, though, remember getting to do my Mae West impression. But it always seems to hang in the air when you don't hear the laugh that usually follows, and the whole movie does that. There's so much comedy, and no laugh track. I remember shooting those scenes, but not too much else." 'Parable of the Rich Man and Lazarus,' came next, and wasn't quite so smooth. "I hated that 'Lazarus Parable' shoot at Grant's Tomb," said Sroka, "and I'm a Northerner! I'm afraid of heights, and I think Gilmer is too, but that didn't stop her from leaning over while she was doing the scene, standing on the very edge of the damned tomb. A sheer drop of many hundreds of feet to the marble floor. They asked me to sit on the ledge with my legs dangling over. Yeah, right, like that's gonna happen. I explained my fear of heights, and they said, 'No worries, we'll put a rope around your waist.' I asked what it would be tied off to, because I knew if I slid off I would take every Greek column with me and we would all end up splattered on top of a dead general. Gilly didn't want a rope. I insisted. She said no. I said, 'I'm going home.' I can't remember whether she was roped or not, but I sure as hell was. I sat there, roped off, sweating, trying not pass out and trying not to look down. They began yelling direction up to us from the ground, but it was too far below, so walkie-talkies were used. All I kept saying into the walkie-talkie was, 'Shoot the damned thing!' And," he finished with a chuckle, "Gilmer loved it. I've never forgiven her." McCormick contended that she was hardly enjoying herself, however. "I guess I would have to say my least favorite scene was the 'Parable of the Rich Man and Lazarus.' On stage, the two characters, Father Abraham and the rich man, had a real connection to each other, even though in context they were a chasm apart. In the film, that chasm was created by putting me atop Grant's Tomb in Riverside Park. That's fine if you pull in your close-up, or even use medium close-up cameras, which is what I thought was happening, when in fact, it wasn't. The cameras stayed in a long shot on me for the entire scene. I was so far away that all my facial expressions, humor and even dialogue were lost. I honestly think that that was the worst scene in the film, poorly conceived and executed, and it was my best scene in the show. It took me a while to get over that, frankly." "It's no secret that I really loved making the film," Lamont added, "but I did feel somewhat disillusioned when we shot the parable about the rich man going to Hades. In the stage version, it's short and sweet, and there's Lazarus above me, and it's a small tableau. In the film, the two perspectives were separated by space and time, and what we were doing in Hades wasn't working for the camera. At the last minute, David Greene decided to have the 'demons' throw pies in my face as the Hades torture. I thought it was a cheap gimmick, and a substitute for a scene that simply didn't work. And for the first time, I worried there might be other such scenes, and that the screen version might not fare as well as we hoped."

It surely must have been a relief, therefore, for all to shoot the next scene, in which Lynne Thigpen would sing "Bless the Lord" at the Central Park Bandshell, its backdrop festooned with silver Mylar. Indeed, the sheer bliss on the faces of the cast as they dance and rejoice to Thigpen's gloriously-rich vocal tones still make it one of the most popular and fun portions of the film, and audiences still respond accordingly. "I spent a lot of time with Sammy constructing the number," Jonas said, "and it was awesome to play in the Bandshell. We had so many onlookers. I remember it was a long day, or even two days, because we had to get the shots of each of us in the silver background. And we'd do it many times, because we'd shoot the girls, who were on one side of the stage, and the boys on the other. I vividly and very fondly remember the intelligence of doing it that way, so it would be more like shooting a stage production in the theater. Working with the girls on the dancing parts was fun. I remember in the end I suggested the choice of Lynne just lifting her leg as opposed to being lifted, based on David's strength. It made a fun comic moment, and it worked." "I don't think anyone could dispute that Lynne Thigpen's gifts were *huge!*" Hanley added. "She was powerfully talented, and a disciplined, intelligent, adorable human being. If she took the stage in *Godspell*, either in the theater or on film at the Bandshell, one couldn't look in another direction. She could belt out a song with so much heart and make you laugh, cry, and sit in wonder, either as an audience member or standing next to her onstage. How could they have cast anyone else?" "When we all got there that morning," recalled McCormick, "Lynne's face was swollen almost double its size!! And she was the lead vocalist that day, of course. We found out that she had been stung by a bee, so antihistamine shots were in order. By the time we were ready to shoot, the swelling was down. But that was a scare. I enjoyed filming that number because we were literally on stage again, so it felt natural and was easy to perform." Lamont concluded, "Lynne worked *really* hard that day."

Then came "All Good Gifts," Merrell Jackson's turn to shine, which would be shot at Central Park's Umpire Rock. "I really enjoyed the days of doing the Central Park scenes," Lamont said. "I was living on West 65th Street at the time, and it felt like doing a movie in my backyard. I also liked the days at Lincoln Center. Overall, though, I think it was the openness of the locations that felt the easiest. As I've said, shooting indoors didn't feel as free." "'All Good Gifts' was always very special to me," said Jonas, "as I had done it with Lamar on stage besides so many 'Lamar clowns' later. And the harmony towards the end, on the word 'loooooooove,' was a sweet connection I had with everyone. I know, it's just a moment, but the whole show/movie is a series of moments, and each one is about making a connection, pushing past ourselves. We all had moments with each other, and this made *Godspell* very special. Either in a skit/parable or in song, it was constructed with an interweaving of all the characters connecting. And I'll always recall that it was a hot, beautiful day in Central Park when we shot that number."

From there came the shot of the entire cast skipping across the Queensborough Bridge (today renamed the Edward I. Koch Bridge) while chanting, "The law and the prophets, the law and the prophets." "Alas for You" came next, shot on the Chelsea Piers long before they were fashionable. "I was living in Chelsea at the time," Hanley recalled, "so just like Robin had the luxury of walking to work when we shot in Central Park and Lincoln Center, I had the same luxury for those one or two days when we shot at the Piers. It was heavenly." "That scene was difficult," said Lansbury, "the scene of the huge Pharisee Monster, which was put together with all kinds of pipes, flexible tubes and platforming." And deep voice of the Monster was provided by none other than John-Michael Tebelak, modulated to sound as fierce and menacing as possible. Tebelak was indeed happy to have an on-screen presence of sorts for the first time in *Godspell's* history, even if some cast members were having a tough go of it with the Monster. "I remember being the mouth of the Pharisee at the pier," Jonas said, "and that was a *very* hot day. There was this clothes dryer exhaust tube we had to hold like an accordion, that we would use to work the Monster's mouth in time with the words. It was a very hot and sweaty experience, with a great deal of physical exertion, much harder even than having to do some of the dances on those hot August days. It was me and somebody else, I honestly don't remember who, awkwardly standing on that ladder thing behind the big face. That was wild, and very grueling." "I don't remember whether or not I was there for the shooting of the Pharisees scene," said Schwartz, "but I feel it is fairly disappointing in its lack of cinematic invention. I still think there was a more imaginative solution."

The 'Parable of the Prodigal Son' sequence, on the other hand, was decidedly eerie for some to shoot for several reasons. For one, it took place at the Cherry Lane Theater, where *Godspell's* initial success began. "That was positively ghostly," said Jonas. Secondly, the action took place in front of a series of clips from silent films, which was both a joy and a nuisance for Alan Heim, who had to work at a dizzy pace to piece it all together properly. Third, it was here that the underscoring of both "Learn Your Lessons Well" and

"We Beseech Thee" would come into play, 'accompanied' by Garber on a dead piano. Sroka, however, was having an absolute ball. "I loved being able to get on the stage where it all started, and what I remember most was David Greene shrieking with laughter while we shot it for those couple of days. He made it easy, for me at least. It was my favorite comedy scene to shoot." "There is a double for me at the end of the Pharisee scene," said McCormick, "because I got very sick, and I was still sick when they shot the Prodigal Son scene, but rather than use a double, they left me out of it completely. You'd have thought that 'Director David' would have taken the time to plug me into that scene somehow, but he didn't. My absence was rather obvious, and many people over the years have commented about it, asking, 'I didn't see you in that scene at the Cherry Lane; where were you?'"

Next on the schedule was "By My Side." "I'll be the first to tell you that that was my favorite scene to shoot," Hanley said. "As I've said, I felt a little disjointed in the Peggy role, and this was my day to step out of the background, away from my roller skates and the clowning, and having license to reveal more emotionally. It was an authentic part of the filming process for me, and I was completely out of myself and just soaring. I will always remember the deep happiness I felt in the midst of that lovely song, and I'll never forget the support I felt from each cast member as I was singing. We had recorded the soundtrack before we filmed, of course, so we were lip-synching each song, and it felt very natural, as we'd been singing together for so many performances prior to filming. There was also one silly thing; when I watch the movie now, I always look for the one part of the song when I'm beginning to move towards Jesus (Victor), stretching my hand towards him, singing, 'I can walk and WALK,' and on that second 'walk' I stumbled into a hole in the grass. I can see on the film how I'm laughing at myself. I was doing all I could to simply walk at that split second. No one noticed, so it made the final cut, and it amuses me."

This was followed by "Beautiful City" which, as stated, not only provided the film with a new song by Schwartz but is also, arguably, the only frame of celluloid where the cast as a whole appear more relaxed than at any other time in the picture. Skipping down Fifth Avenue, then into Lincoln Center and around Bethesda Fountain in pairs and triples, their smiles are as wide as the Grand Canyon while they sing. The only applicable way to describe the atmosphere would be one of visibly carefree abandon, which completely projects off the screen. "Mostly it was a chance to dance, to skip through the city," Jonas said. "The largest part was skipping in a circle at Lincoln Center in a wide open area, as I recall, with the camera in the center moving in the opposite direction as we sang, skipped and did schtick with each other, usually created on the fly. A lot of the movie had this flexible improv thing about it, because we never knew what we were going to deal with until we were there at the location."

The last scene to be shot in daylight, and another of the rare few that took more than two days to complete, was the joyous "Light of the World." Set aboard a tugboat that traveled around the East River and the Statue of Liberty, here Judas and the Disciples are transformed into the crew of a ship, with Jesus as the skipper. And to the audience, the sense of camaraderie among the cast is never more palpable as when they mime rowing the boat while Garber barks "Stroke!" repeatedly into a megaphone, his lithe physicality being forced backwards at every call and forward move of the vessel. "This, to me, was the most fun scene of all to shoot," said Hanley. "I grew up near Lake Michigan, on Chicago's North Shore, so I feel the most alive when I'm near water. And to think up improvisations on a funny old tugboat, looking at New York City, circling the Statue of Liberty, enjoying drinking wine with that adorable group of people even if it was the cheap stuff, and getting paid for that experience, was simply *it* for me!" Lamont agreed, "Being on the tugboat was a hoot! Again, it felt like the right locale for the song; there was just something about being on the water, the breeze blowing, and the city drifting by on the shore. It gave you a sense of being separate from the noise and concrete of Manhattan, and yet being close to it." For Sroka, unfortunately, fun was the last word he'd have used to describe the experience. "During the tugboat sequence, I was sick as a dog," he said. "I overslept, was late getting to the set, didn't eat, and took several Sudafed. Then I got seasick, and I was throwing up between takes. Every time we did a take, David Greene wanted a specific background of Manhattan behind us. So we'd do a take, and the damn tugboat would have to make a huge circle, come back to the start mark, and begin again.

Let's just say that this is *really* special if you're seasick. Although, if you watch the scenes today, I don't think you can tell how miserable I was feeling. As a side note, there were no props to use in the wheelhouse, so I grabbed the binocular holders and just improvised with them, which worked pretty well."

The remaining scenes, which built to the film's climax, were all shot at night on Ward's Island. These include the Last Supper and Betrayal by Judas, "On the Willows," (in an extremely-moving tableaux with Jesus removing each Disciple's makeup and a tearful-but-jubilant goodbye to one and all), and the Crucifixion. Again, all of these were shot in the precise order in which they would appear in the finished film. "Shooting in sequence, for the most part," said Lamont, "also brought the cast and crew together in a nice way. At first, some of the crew members were skeptical of us and the entire project; many had come from working on films with established stars and a much more traditional setup. Now, they were working with inexperienced kids on a project that felt a little too hippy-dippy and Christian. Over time, however, we developed a camaraderie that was very nice, at least for me. I got along with everyone and enjoyed talking at breaks with the grips, and set assistants. And by the end, when we shot the Betrayal and Crucifixion, it was a night shoot in early fall, cold and dark. Whenever David Greene would yell 'Cut!' several crew members would run out and cover us with coats while we sat waiting for the next shot, or to do it over again. I do think some of the crew was moved by the scene, and their kindness came not simply from having worked with us for a few months, but because of the nature of the film." "It really was a sad time," Hanley said, "because we knew that our experience was coming to an end. When we were looping the film, as I said, we watched it in black-and-white. During the Crucifixion scene, the entire cast was sobbing, partly because we all knew it was almost over, and partly because seeing it without color was so powerful; removing the color took some of the grandeur out of the production, getting it back to its intimate roots, and restoring the ominous connection between the cast, the message, and the audience. *Godspell* is a generous show, after all. It involves the audience in a way that delights and rewards." Lansbury added, "We also had problems on the very last Crucifixion scene, because the sun was going down on the East River. Since this scene is supposed to take place at dawn, I suggested we film the sun going down, and then reverse it to appear as if it was rising. I think that worked fairly well."

And there it was. Jesus was cut down from the cyclone fence, paraded through the empty streets upon the shoulders of the cast singing "Long Live God" and "Prepare Ye" in counterpoint, the sun once again rose upon New York City, and the corner of Park and 68th teemed with people untouched by the Almighty, before the credits rolled and an organ solo by Paul Shaffer encompassed the final reprise of "Day by Day," with the handclaps that had proved so painful to the cast while recording the soundtrack. *Godspell* had been completed once and for all as a film. Whether or not there was actually a 'wrap party' isn't readily remembered. "There must have been one, but I don't recall anything about it that stands out," said Jonas, while Lamont said, "If there was, I'm pretty sure I wasn't there." Hanley said, "There was definitely a party, but I don't think it was on the set. I seem to remember that it was at someone's apartment, but I can't remember who. What I *do* remember is that Jerry had us all laughing hysterically all night, doing impersonations and funny voices." "Maybe I was there in spirit," said Sroka, "but I don't recall." "There may have been one, but I know I wasn't there," said McCormick. And Garber said, "Maybe my invitation got lost in the mail or something. I can't remember back that far."

Godspell sailed through post-production, although everyone wasn't always necessarily thinking soberly. Editor Alan Heim said, "Every evening in the cutting room, at about 5 PM, David Greene would take out a pouch of grass, roll a joint, and offer me a toke. Though I smoked at the time, I would refuse because I felt it would cloud my judgment. He poo-poohed my fears, saying he had smoked for so many years it never affected him. And, sure enough, the decisions we made in the evening were always fine the next morning."

On the afternoon of March 20, 1973, Edgar Lansbury was having lunch at Lincoln Center with John Van Eyssen, the intrepid production chief for Columbia Pictures in the UK. Joining them was Van Eyssen's longtime lady-companion Ingrid Bergman, and her daughters, Pia Lindstrom and Isabella Rossellini. This wouldn't normally be considered extraordinary, but for the fact that *Godspell* would have its premiere later that evening, just steps from where the group of five was seated. "That was a fun lunch, I must say," said Lansbury. "The premiere was being held as the centerpiece of the Lincoln Center Film Festival." And McCormick agreed that it was a very exciting evening. "We 'dressed in our finest linen,' and went to this grand event at Lincoln Center. There were a great many people there that night, Angela Lansbury and Patrick MacGoohan among them, and though the night is another sort of blur, my impression is that the film was warmly received." "All I remember thinking," said Jonas, "was that I didn't like what I was wearing. Silly, right? But I can tell you that we were treated like royalty. It was awesome." Garber said, "The premiere was terribly exciting. The thing I remember most was my divorced parents meeting in an elevator at the hotel, where they were both staying, and trying to be civil. But everything turned out fine." Sroka added, "I wore my green velvet wedding suit. It was an exciting night, with the press asking questions to the wrong people, since nobody knew who we were. My parents came in from New Jersey, and were very proud." "The whole thing was just so opulent," Hanley recalled, "with spotlights going back and forth, red carpet and all. I remember my grandmother coming with my parents, telling people, as we walked in, 'I'm Katie Hanley's grandmother!' and feeling horrified. It was an exciting night, and yes, my parents were very proud. Honestly, *Godspell* gave each of us moments to shine, but we shone brightest as a group, and we knew the message was contagious. It was a great feeling to have been part of it." Reinhardt said, "I loved seeing my wife Gilmer as a hot blonde! I loved the frozen people stepping out of time, and the empty streets of New York, but I remember thinking that the city itself dwarfed the intimacy of the work—the wonderful small moments that peppered the stage show. What I really loved were all the new musical moments—underscoring and connectives that I had been at the recording session for, but had no idea how they were going to play. And I loved 'All for the Best.' I thought it was the best conception in the movie." "They invited me," said Peggy Gordon, "but I decided not to go. I was much happier to stay out of the spotlight and let Katie enjoy it. But I did see the film in San Francisco when it opened there, and it was disheartening, because there were literally six people in the entire movie theater." "My memory is that there was a premiere at Lincoln Center and I did attend," said Schwartz. "I remember there was stressfulness in whether or not the final print would be ready in time, and I remember working on the sound in the theater for the premiere and not being entirely happy with it; I may have made the sound too loud."

The next day, when the film opened nationwide on March 21, all involved might well have been singing, "We beseech thee, hear us!!" Because the best of times and the worst of times were just around the corner, in more ways than one for more than one person; the dawning of the age of Aquarius was hardly on the horizon.

PART THREE: LEARN YOUR LESSONS WELL

As was the custom of the day in New York, Vincent Canby led the pack of the press brigade when his review was published in the *Times* on March 22:

"In filling in some of the narrative gaps in the Gospel According to St. Mark, St. Matthew took pains with the chronology, which, if you read him closely, makes it seem as if Jesus, on the day after He delivered the Sermon on the Mount and effected three healings, was in such good form that He made two lake crossings, healed five more people and held several lengthy discussions.

"It is this quality of nonstop busy-ness that is one of the chief assets of *Godspell*, both of the Off-Broadway musical (still running at the Promenade Theater on upper Broadway) and of the film adaptation that opened yesterday at the Columbia 2 Theater. Especially of the film. This update of—and variation on—the Gospel According to St. Matthew is less a celebration of the life and teachings of Christ than it is a celebration of theater, music, youthful high spirits, New York City locations and the zoom lens. The movie amounts to one long, breathless production number (some of whose parts are considerably less effective than others), as well as a demonstrations that, in films, what is said is often less important than how it's said.

"*Godspell* pretty much reduces the story of Jesus to conform to a kind of flower-child paranoia that was probably more popular three or four years ago than it is today: the only way to survive in this world is to drop out of it, which, if you think about it, effectively reverses Jesus' instructions to the disciples.

"That, however, is to mistake what I, at least, understand *Godspell* to be all about. It's not about religion or philosophy but show business, and its frame—the life and death of Jesus re-enacted in contemporary Manhattan and environs—is hardly more than a gimmick to allow the show's authors to help themselves to some lovely original material never protected by copyright.

"At its worst, *Godspell* exalts a kind of simplicity and sweetness that are often the disguises of fierce anti-intellectualism. Luckily, the film constantly betrays itself through its highly sophisticated show-biz manners. Jesus is not simply the androgynous circus clown He looks to be. As played by Victor Garber, He's a tireless hoofer and a most engaging minstrel man. One of the finest production numbers I've seen in years is the exuberant and ironic 'All for the Best,' which Jesus and John the Baptist (David Haskell) sing and dance all over New York, highlighted by a marvelous soft-shoe done in front of the Bulova Watch sign overlooking Times Square.

"After a certain point, all of Stephen Schwartz's music begins to sound the same, but there is a momentum in its pacing that carries us over the monotony. Almost every member of the cast has his or her moment of glory at screen center. I think particularly of Robin Lamont, a beautiful honey-blonde, who sings "Day by Day," and of several hugely funny parables acted out by virtually the entire company.

"John-Michael Tebelak, who is credited with having 'conceived and staged' the Off-Broadway show, is credited as associate director of the film, and David Greene as its director. I have no idea who did what, but the movie has the look of something shot by Richard Lester in an evangelical frame of mind. Ordinarily, this sort of fractured style is something I can easily resist, but it is the only way, I suspect, that *Godspell* could be made to work on film.

"Every song number is an amalgam of splintery shots against dozens of New York locations, and a lot of them are both funny and beautiful. I can't remember another film that seems to have caught the way New York appears on a lot of hot summer days, when its jagged outlines are softened by a golden smog. The atmosphere may be lethal, but it's also incomparably romantic.

"I have some of these same feelings of ambivalence about *Godspell*. I like its music, its drive and its determination, even when it's pretending to a kind of innocence and naiveté that I never for a second believe."

Meanwhile, Roger Ebert published the following in the *Chicago Sun-Times* the day before, on March 21:

"The thing about *Godspell* that caught my heart was its simplicity, its refusal to pretend to be anything more than it is. It's not a message for our times, or a movie to cash in on the Jesus movement, or even quite a youth movie. It's a series of stories and songs, like the Bible is, and it's told with the directness that simple stories need: with no tricks, no intellectual gadgets, and a lot of openness.

"This was the quality that attracted me to the stage version. I had to be almost dragged to the play, because its subject matter sounded so depressingly contemporary. But after I finally got into the theater and sat down and let *Godspell* relax me, I found myself simply letting it happen. For a musical based on the Gospel according to St. Matthew, *Godspell* is strangely irreverent, wacky, and endearing.

"The stage version has been opened up into a movie by taking the whole of New York as a set. Except for the scenes at the beginning and end—which show the city as a temple of mammon and a rat nest—the movie is populated only by its cast; we don't see anybody else, and the ten kids dance, sing, and act out parables in such unlikely places as the World Trade Center and a tugboat. This is a new use for New York, which looks unusually clean; even its tacky skyscrapers edge toward grandeur when the vast long shots engulf them.

"Against this wilderness of steel and concrete, the characters come on like kids at a junior high reunion, clothed in comic book colors and bright tattered rags. Only two have names: Jesus, and a character who plays both John (who ushered Jesus into the Bible) and Judas (who hastened him out). The other eight characters, who seem to represent an on-the-spot gathering of disciples, are just themselves.

"What's nice about the casting—which gives us all new faces—is that the characters don't look like professional stage youths. Remember *West Side Story*, where all the allegedly teenage dancers looked like hardened theatrical professionals in greaser wigs? *Godspell*'s cast is not only young but is allowed to look like a collection of individuals. These could conceivably be real people, and their freshness helps put the material over even when it seems pretty obvious. For some blessed reason the director, David Greene, has resisted any temptation to make the movie visually fancy. With material of this sort, there must have been an impulse to go for TV-commercial trendiness, but Greene's style is unforced, and goes well with the movie's freshness and basic colors.

"The movie characters, like the stage characters, are given little watercolor designs on their faces by Jesus. A girl gets a little yellow flower, a boy gets a tiny red star, and so on. It was necessary in the stage version to exaggerate this makeup to make it visible, but the movie underplays it and it was gentle and nice. It occurred to me, about an hour into the film, that maybe young people will pick up on this. Tattoos were big in the '70s—little butterflies and stars—so why not face-paint zigzags and pinwheels and flowers? Anything to brighten up this miserable world: Which is what *Godspell* is saying, anyway. "

On balance, these reviews may not have been unequivocal raves, but they also weren't out-and-out hate letters. In fact, other early reviews were even more positive. And then Richard Schickel of *Time* magazine absolutely ripped the movie apart on April 5:

"*Godspell* is a little time capsule of a movie. Some day archaeologists will dig it up and reconstruct from this all-singing, all-dancing version of the Gospel according to Consciousness III much of what was shoddy about American culture (cinema subdivision) in the last half of the twentieth century.

"Responding to mysterious sci-fi bleepings, a group of flower children led by David Haskell come together for a splash party in Central Park's Belvedere Fountain. There they find Christ: an androgyne wearing a Superman sweatshirt. Repairing to a junkyard, which handles only clean and cute junk, they outfit themselves as a band of strolling players devoted to acting out the Passion against the picturesque backdrop of the modern Jerusalem (Manhattan!). The players hop, skip and bounce relentlessly through their routines as if the relevant saint for them was St. Vitus. Not that any of these rolling pebbles bring any passion to the Passion, since what they want to elicit from the audience is a series of ahs rather than a sense of awe. Nor that New York, in Director David Greene's vision, looks like a city in need of salvation—which it surely is.

"Indeed, the need being so obvious and the city's tawdriness such a familiar symbol of the nation's urban mess, each Saran-wrapped view of it is likely to jar audiences with a shock of non-recognition. Where has Greene hidden the psychologically bombed civilian population? Where have all the smog, graffiti and litter gone?

"Still, the blame for turning the viewer's idle mind into a devil's workshop of speculation is not entirely Greene's. The author of the original hit play, John-Michael Tebelak, collaborated with him on a screenplay that finds no equivalent in hippie jargon for the exalted language of the Bible. Instead it offers, among other conceits, the Lazarus legend climaxed with a pie in the face. Stephen Schwartz's score is perfectly suited to this level of imitation rock. 'God save the people/Save the people from despair,' one of Schwartz's lyrics moans. A good beginning would have been to spare them *Godspell*, which adores him far less than it does its own adorableness."

Schwartz said, "I remember of course being disappointed that the reviews weren't better. In those days, I still hadn't learned not to read reviews—it wasn't until about a year later that I finally realized how destructive it was to me to read reviews of my own work, positive or negative, and stopped reading them. I remember being particularly annoyed at Richard Schickel for nastily criticizing my lyrics for 'Save the People,' when of course I hadn't written them; they were from the Episcopal hymnal and written probably a century or so previously. I remember being stunned at seeing such a clear factual error in print. Needless to say, nowadays I would no longer be stunned." Lansbury, on the other hand, said, "I've been in the theatre too long to be affected by reviews. Most of the ones for the film were quite good, as I recall." "I don't read reviews," said Victor Garber, "but someone told me that Vincent Canby referred to me as a 'hoofer,' which made me laugh and still does." "I remember reading the Times review," said Reinhardt, "which seemed like one of those reviews that wouldn't hurt the film. By that time, the show and the subject matter had become iconic, so I seem to remember the reviews were mixed, and for the same reasons I had doubts from the beginning, about successfully capturing that '*Godspell* magic' I've talked about. The feeling among the cast was that the movie failed in that respect." McCormick said, "I really don't remember any of the reviews, but I do know that when I saw the film for the first time at the premiere, I didn't experience even remotely the impact that the stage show had on me the first time I saw it. My impression is that the reviewers said basically the same thing. Although one amusing thing that I recall was, we all thought it was a laugh that the movie takes place over a period of one day, because if you look carefully from the beginning of the movie to the last, we all must have gained at least five pounds during shooting. You get great eats on a movie set." "I don't really even remember the reviews, except for Gene Shalit's, because I think I still have a copy," said Lamont. "He wasn't strong on the film, but mentioned as one of the highlights the 'beautiful honey blonde' who sang 'Day By Day.' I was immensely flattered."

Hanley wasn't surprised by the reviews. "*Godspell* is powerful when performed in a small theatre. When the show was done right, as Stephen Schwartz always reminded us, each clown is genuinely listening to the Jesus clown. If 'show biz ego' strikes one actor, drawing focus, then the well is poisoned. Childlike wonder, reverence, and the desire to be teachable and listen is a must for *Godspell* to work. I remember one actor hearing about an agent who was going to be in the audience one night, and he started drawing attention to himself and overdoing things. The show didn't work as well that night, and Stephen set us all straight as to why. *Godspell* is meant to be intimate. Each funny and touching exchange is caught and appreciated to the fullest by the audience in a small theatre. To blow this show up onto the big screen seems to dilute it. Those of us who performed in smaller theatres witnessed rabbis and nuns standing to their feet, cheering, with tears streaming down their faces at the curtain call. I'm sure glad that I got to be part of the film, but always felt that I'd experienced *Godspell* at its finest on a smaller scale." Peggy Gordon wasn't surprised either. "My first reaction was that David Greene's concept of a city empty of people, as opposed to John-Michael's concept of an empty world, was upstaging. It was like a travelogue of all the most beautiful places to visit in New York. Even the junkyard was clean and filled with fun stuff. So, for me, regardless of whether the reviews were fair, the 'show' was lost in all the scenery. But, over the years, when I've seen it on television, I feel it does translate, even though 'By My Side,' technically, makes no sense in that new context. The lyrics are all about that one clown empowering herself to go with him—period. In the context David Greene created, Jesus is upset by the encounter with the Pharisees and they are essentially comforting *him* by telling him they'll always be by his side. I loved what Katie did, even though she told me how disjointed it felt. She kept it simple, real and heartfelt; but I always giggle because if you really listen to the lyrics, it kind of doesn't make sense. So, I felt the reviews were probably accurate, at first glance."

Regardless of whether *Godspell* was emerging as the same critical success as its counterpart on stage, the film was selected to open the 1973 Cannes Film Festival. Not only would Lansbury, Beruh, Greene, Tebelak and Schwartz and select other production staff be attending, but so would Garber, Haskell and Lamont. "Columbia flew us to Cannes," Lamont recalled, "where they put us up at what is now the Intercontinental Carleton, which was magnificent. We got a kick out of the dining room, which had formal waiters and sommeliers hovering all the time. Our first dinner there, Jeannie Haskell (David's wife) ordered a fish appetizer and a fish entrée. The waiter seemed hesitant to place her order, after explaining that one simply did not do that. Hey, we were young, and very uncouth. The hotel was just down the street from the Palais du Festival, where the films were shown. *Godspell* was to be the opening film, and we were whisked down the street by limousine. When we got out, there was a wall of photographers lining the steps up to the Palais, and it was absolutely overwhelming. There was a dinner afterwards, and I remember being seated next to the Minister of Culture of France. I spoke a bit of French, but it was difficult to communicate. From Cannes, we flew to London for the opening of the film there, and then flew to Los Angeles for the opening in LA. It was a real whirlwind trip." "Of course," Schwartz added, "I also very fondly remember the trip to Cannes, which was an amazing experience for someone still in his mid-twenties." Lansbury also remembered, "Columbia took the entire company to Cannes and put us up in the hotels on the Croisette. The film opened the Festival, but it was not in competition. There were lots of celebrities and hoopla, of course. At the screening, the audience was making a lot of noise when the film started, which was very rude of them, and David Greene actually stood up, turned around, and screamed at them to shut up! Which they did. This was followed by a lavish dinner, and then David left early for the opening in Los Angeles while the rest of us went on to London." Sroka added, "When David Greene returned from the French premiere in Paris, he told me to pack and move there immediately, because of the Parisian response when my picture came up during the credits."

When all was said and done, the film ended up far from being a moneymaker at the box office. The exact gross and net aren't known or remembered, although the film did recoup its initial investment of $1.3 milion. Bruce Nash, of the Beverly Hills firm Nash Information Services, which is arguably the film industry's leading expert in revenue research, can only find that according to the January 9, 1980 edition of *Variety*, which published a list of every film to earn over $4 million in domestic theater rentals, *Godspell* was not on that list. Thus, one can imply that the total domestic box office for the film was less than $8 million. Common theory is that the film was hurt by the nearly-simultaneous release of *Jesus Christ Superstar*, with its higher budget and more concentrated publicity machine. Others contend that it was simply too difficult for a film like *Godspell* to possibly compete with such other heavy hitters of the day as *Paper Moon, American Graffiti, The Exorcist, Last Tango in Paris, The Sting, The Way We Were* and *Cries and Whispers*.

However, time has been far more kind to the film than critics and audiences during its initial release; it is still broadcast on television annually as an Easter special, the soundtrack continues to sell, and not once in nearly four decades has the movie not continued to garner a whole new generation of fans while retaining its original fan base. Just a cursory look at the reader reviews on websites like Amazon and IMDB yields hundreds of positive feedback from *Godspell* lovers all over the world, from longtime followers and new ones. This is not to say that the film doesn't still have its detractors, both professional journalists and members of the public sector who opt to post their negativity online. There's even a pro-Christian website with a page decrying the film as "the ULTIMATE blasphemy" and calling for fire and brimstone to rid the earth of the heathens who would have created such a horrible display, which inadvertently only serves to increase *Godspell*'s following. As if none of this was enough, a group of die-hard fans of the film, students at Dartmouth, developed a *Godspell* Drinking Game in 2001, in which participants must take a shot of liquor when a certain action takes place on the screen (these include Hanley jumping headfirst into the fountain, Mylett trilling the "rrrrrrrr" sound on the word "priest" in the Parable of the Good Samaritan, and when Nina Faso appears at the very end, coming around the corner with the rest of New York).

Robin Lamont's favorite example of a fan reaching out to her, in a happenstance that she rightfully claims makes her extremely proud, was in an e-mail she received in 2010, from an anonymous American soldier who had been stationed in Iraq:

"We were a Combat Support Hospital unit that was augmenting another CSH at the main hospital site in Baghdad (we'd captured Saddam's old hospital and took over operation of it in 2003). Our job was to care for the wounded soldiers and Marines in our area of responsibility (AOR), which extended from The Syrian border in the west to the Iranian border to our east, as for north as Baquba and as far south as Karbala.

"I lived in a dorm-like building on the hospital campus, and had become friends with a few soldiers from the other unit who liked to go up to the roof of our 'hootch' and hang out a few evenings a week. We'd sit in lawn chairs, drink a little black market rum and coke (never enough to get drunk, just enough to chill out a bit) and listen to music. The rule was that everyone brought a few tunes to contribute, things we really enjoyed, not just background music. The more obscure the better. Our perch had a great view of southeastern Baghdad, which is actually a very pretty part of town (if you can look past the destruction), overlooking the helicopter landing pad to the west and the Tigris River to the east. Sadr City, the infamous slum that Muqtada al-Sadr's Mahdi Army had roared out of on Good Friday that year, was just across the river and back a half mile. We took mortar and rocket fire out of there daily, often at night while we were up on the roof, providing us with spectacular fireworks displays and a bit of excitement once in a while.

"On the night I want to describe, it was a gorgeous mid-May evening, about eighty degrees and balmy, with a warm, gentle breeze out of the west and a million stars above us (maybe a million and three, it's hard to remember). It was my turn to DJ, and I had just downloaded a long-missed treasure off the Internet that I was eager to share with the crew. We topped off our drinks, sat back to watch a helicopter full of wounded soldiers departing for Germany by way of Balad (a town to our north with an airfield), and watched a flaming orange sun settle into the horizon as the sky turned a million shades of purple and blue. It had been busy that day patient-wise, and we were all a little frayed around the edges and needing some mental healing.

"I queued up 'Beautiful City' for them and sat back to watch their reactions.

"War does funny things to people immersed in it. Sometimes it makes you bitter, or cynical, or angry. Sometimes things that would normally make you smile, don't. Things that you'd never worry about fill you with blinding rage. Suffering that would make a statue cry don't phase you. And sometimes, a sweet, silly song from a thirty-year-old musical makes you smile.

"I'm sure when you were filming that song in New York City all those many years ago, none of you imagined that four scared and homesick soldiers caught up in the madness of a war in the desert would ever listen to it and feel better, if only for a few minutes, but it happened. We all saw the city we were in, an ancient and yet modern city struggling to rebuild itself after the onslaught of the American war machine and decades of abuse and terror under Saddam Hussein, in a different way that evening. We saw past the crumbled buildings, shell craters and broken windows, and saw a beautiful city that we'd had all around us for so long but had never noticed before. The white stucco walls, the orchids and roses and other dazzling flowers that nobody knew the names of, the tree-lined boulevards, the shadowed fronds of the date palms. It was shocking how a song none of them had ever heard before had lifted a curtain from before their eyes, revealing a side of their existence that had been hidden.

"After the song ended I sat quietly, waiting for their response. Normally we were a pretty talkative bunch, telling stories that corresponded with our song choices, like, "I saw this song played live on a beach in Hawaii," or "I heard this one the first time I got laid," or whatever. But I kept quiet. The *Godspell* story, as you well know, is not a brief tale, and I didn't want to monopolize the conversation. So we sat silently, each looking into the distance, lost in thought, for a moment or two. It was a moment I'll never forget, nor will they. It was interrupted by a rocket that sailed right over our heads and forced us to flee the rooftop, but that was OK too. We'd gotten our break, and that was all we could ask for."

Stephen Schwartz tries valiantly today to stay positive when reminiscing about the film and how it all turned out. "I was fairly involved with the conceptualization of the movie, particularly the idea of the magically-empty New York, and the *Wizard of Oz*-like opening and closing sequences. I know that a couple of sequences in musical numbers were my idea, particularly some of the locations for 'All for the Best,' such as filming in front of the Accutron sign. I remember pushing for the movie to have the kind of anarchic and youthful energy of Richard Lester's *A Hard Day's Night*, which I still wish there were more of in the film. Beyond that, my impression of my responsibilities was that I would be in charge of the music, as with the stage show. I will say that I wished then, and still wish, that the city had seemed more magically empty, with wider shots that would make one wonder how they were achieved. I remember being disappointed by the relatively brief establishing shots of the de-populated New York in the opening, and asking if there could be more of them and if they could last longer. I felt the mysteriousness of the concept could have been more strongly established if we'd done that. For the most part I was happy with David Greene's casting decisions, and I particularly thought the choice of Victor Garber was a good one, as I had been a big fan of his performance in Toronto. I'm not sure that the final cast is entirely the one I would have assembled if it had been completely up to me, but it was never questioned that it was and should be the director's decision. I wouldn't ever use the word 'disillusioned,' to describe how I felt about the finished film, but I remember during the editing process, when I helped put together 'All for the Best' and 'Light of the World,' being disappointed there wasn't more coverage to draw from. I wanted to use a lot more cuts, and we just didn't have the footage to do it.

"While I feel for several reasons this was not the best possible film adaptation of *Godspell*, and a film adaptation of such a highly theatrical show is obviously difficult to pull off under the best of circumstances, I guess I'm most proud of the imaginativeness of the concept, though as I've said, I do wish it had been more fully realized cinematically. And I guess I'm proud of the fact that it still speaks to many people all these years later, even though it's so much a movie of its time. And," he continued, "while I liked David Greene very much as a person and think he was a very skilled director of excellent television dramas, I feel he never really 'got' the show, and consequently the spirit of the film version didn't really capture the essence. I think he misunderstood the urban 'clowns' of the show as being hippie-esque 'flower children,' and thus missed a lot of the subversive humor. Maybe it was because he was British, and the British point of view towards this story is more *Jesus Christ Superstar* than *Godspell* although, as I say, I think the British director Richard Lester had the cinematic style I feel might have worked better for the film. But David and everyone else involved were certainly devoted to the project and pleasant to work with; I remember no personality conflicts or any of the behind-the-scenes clashes that can mar other experiences."

Gilmer McCormick takes far less pleasure in remembering the moviemaking experience overall. "At the beginning, as we were going into rehearsals, I was a little apprehensive and a whole lot curious as to how we were going to pull this off. I expected 'talk-throughs' with David Greene, but that never happened. It was as if we were expected to just keep on doing what we had been doing on stage and that would be OK. But it wasn't, and we all knew it wasn't. There's a big difference between acting for the stage and acting for the screen, and especially with material whose central characters are clowns. You have to pull it in, make it smaller without hopefully losing the power. An actor relies on his director to help make this adjustment, and David Greene was out of his element with that. The most helpful and insightful director on set was Sammy Bayes. He was very careful to align his choreography with the characters who were dancing it, and I think the numbers are the best parts of the movie. They were true to the spirit and the characters of the piece, and the days we danced were my happiest. So the movie experience as a whole, for me, was not a good one, and I think that was mainly because of the choice of director, although I had greatly admired his work in other films. David Greene was an elderly, rather eccentric Englishman who, again, I think just found himself outside his element, and justifiably so. *Godspell*, after all, comes out of American Street Theatre, which is very hard to translate to the screen, unless you're Martin Scorcese, which he was not. The screen wants to narrow the focus and the stage wants to expand the focus, and part of the success and charm of *Godspell* was its expansiveness.

"To add to what was already said, I have to be honest when I say that Greene was very temperamental on the set. He appeared frustrated a lot of the time, often disappearing into his trailer or a nearby secluded area for sometimes longer than the normal break would allow, leaving us wondering what was wrong. That sense of insecurity made its rounds more than once, and if it hadn't been for Steve Schwartz and John-Michael besides Sammy, I don't know what we would have done. They were the steady hands on the keel, and helped us keep our eyes on the ball. But," she continued, "although I think the sheer impact of *Godspell* was lost a little in translation going from stage to film, the fact is, it succeeded on other levels that in many ways are the most important levels. That the movie continues to inspire new generations says a lot for the impact it actually did have, and continues to have. I still receive fan mail from people whose lives the film has touched or changed in some way, and I know that John-Michael intended to change lives when he wrote *Godspell* in the first place. And as an older person now, I look at the film with entirely new eyes, and it's almost like flipping through an album. All the good times rise to the top and all the bad times just seem to fade away."

"What I think people most need to remember, and this was something of which I had to remind myself every single day when the process began," said Joanne Jonas, "is that the show and the film are apples and oranges. We were not making a movie of the show, and there is no way the two would or could possibly have been similar, aside from the score and the costumes. They were two completely separate experiences. And all I wanted and hoped was that the film would be liked, which it was and still is. I certainly never realized it would become this big cult hit, or that people would watch it on Easter the way other people watch *It's a Wonderful Life* at Christmas. And I very much enjoyed working with David. The simple fact is," she added, "I am a *Godspell*ian, true and true. I loved all aspects of working on this classic, and am very proud to say I was in both the original off-Broadway show *and* the movie. I was the youngest of the group when we started the show, I was just turning twenty-one, and so I lacked maturity and experience. But in my favor, I had an innocence and wisdom beyond my years. Like me or not, there are thousands of people, young and old, who appreciated what we did, and are still writing to me asking my opinion and advice on all aspects of *Godspell* and acting, so something is there, everlasting. Many 'Joanne clowns' have written asking me what I felt 'her' essence was/is, and I gladly give my opinion. She is born from me, and will forever be called Joanne."

"Overall and in retrospect, yes, the entire shoot was difficult," Victor Garber said, "but the fun came, as it usually does, from the cast joining together in what seemed to be an impossible task. It was my first film, and I had no idea how arduous, and exhausting, filmmaking was. Shooting a movie in New York, which is supposed to be uninhabited, was somewhat of a nightmare. However, I know that *Godspell* had a huge impact on a great many people, and I am happy to be a part of that. For me, it was really a tremendous learning experience, and often I am stopped on the street by fans of the show and thanked for my participation." He added, "It's odd that in this business, you can have such an intense, intimate experience with so many people, and then completely lose contact. It never ceases to amaze me. I loved everyone in that movie and, probably, a lot of that came from the part, and the relationship I had with each individual. It was definitely a life-changing role for me. I probably should have cut my hair immediately after the film came out, but I held onto the afro, until I realized I had to let it all go. It was definitely time to move on."

Jerry Sroka said, "I can't possibly say anything else that I haven't already said. I loved making the movie, I loved David Greene, and I loved and will always love *Godspell* and everybody involved. I wasn't able to make it to the fortieth reunion, but I'll be damned if I don't make it to the fiftieth. And I'd love to be able to share it all with David Greene. You know, I ran into him on the street in Santa Monica several years ago. I could tell it was David from the back; oh, that wild hair! I walked up behind him and in my silliest Southern voice, I whispered, 'I said, kill it!!!' Without turning, David whispered, 'Oh, my God, Jerry Sroka.' We stood on the corner and talked for a long time, and agreed that *Godspell* was the high point in both of our professional lives."

"In retrospect, it was quite amazing that David Greene ever even saw me onstage to begin with," said Katie Hanley. "I was in the original cast of *Grease* in New York then, as well as an understudy for *Godspell*. I'd been in the second cast of *Godspell*, when the original cast went to Los Angeles to open the show. At that time I was the Robin clown, singing 'Day by Day.' David had seen the show at the Promenade several times, but happened to go one more time the night I was called in to understudy Peggy's 'By My Side' clown. I got my understudy to go on in *Grease*, as I had a strong loyalty and devotion to *Godspell*. David told me that when he saw me sing that night he knew he would cast me in the film. I will never forget the moment he said that. And it's amazing to think that if I hadn't gone on that night, there's a very good chance I wouldn't be here right now telling this story. Also, the original *Godspell* cast members were, for the most part, a band of geniuses. Through improvisations, amazing wit and humor, talent, heart, and dedication, their gifts brought *Godspell* to all of us. And I think the world is better for it." She continued, "After filming, David Greene wrote personal thank-you letters to each one in the cast. I have mine in my scrapbook. He told me the particular moments he loved from my performance, and it was so much like him to take the time to do that. When I first saw him—tall, wild white hair, jeans, with Converse shoes—I was intimidated and amused. The only men I'd seen who were his age wore suits and overcoats with briefcases, at least in Chicago. At first, I thought that David was dressing the way he did, and wearing his wild hair that way, in order to help us to identify with him. But when I last saw him, in his eighties, he was dressed exactly the same way; he was elegant hippie royalty. His booming voice could silence an unruly crowd in a split second, and his laugh was the largest and most distinctive I've ever heard. I can hear it now. He was a powerhouse and a gentle spirit. When filming was over, and I'd received his generous thank-you note, I took out my daughter's crayons and drew a childish cartoon of each of our clowns and mailed it to him. The last time I saw him, at a reunion in Los Angeles in 2001, he showed me a photograph he'd taken of my drawing, telling me that it was hanging in a frame on his 'wall of accomplishments' at home, right next to a picture of him directing Bette

Davis in a television film. Just before he passed away, I called to tell him about the passing of Lynne Thigpen. He told me that it saddened him deeply to hear that, but also grieved him to tell me that he, too, was dying. I am so honored to have worked with him, and his kind words shaped how I perceived myself."

"David Greene was one of those people, and especially one of those directors," Sammy Bayes said, "who will always be thought of by different people in different ways. What I can tell you is that he was excellent to work with. There was always discussion and exchanging ideas on how to approach a scene, and he was open to any thoughts I had, regardless of which scene or number it was. It seems odd to think of him as humble, but he was, in his way. It wasn't all about, 'I'm the director, so we're doing it this way and there'll be no discussion,' it was, 'Sammy, thank you, that idea is brilliant, and let's do it.' What he wanted more than anything from his creative staff was that we keep his creative vision moving forward. One of the most gracious gifts he gave me personally was his invitation to sit in on the editing sessions with him and Alan Heim, and work together with them on any musical number I staged or choreographed. This was a tremendous gift, as it taught me so much about media. Every day, from my first on *Godspell* to the last, was a positive experience. And that I credit to David's way of working with his people, and always trusting their judgment. He really respected what we brought to the table, and it showed both on the screen and off."

"I just felt and feel proud that I had been connected with it," said Alan Heim, "and that I felt we had made the best possible film of the show. Especially because there was a lot of footage David told me he hadn't known what to do with, and we really found ways to use it all. Almost any film, made any time and with any cast, is a good thing simply because it is something to be left for posterity. It lives on, with or without you. With *Godspell*, I enjoyed the whole process of working on the film, and had great relationships with David and with Edgar Lansbury. I was to work with David on his next project, which was cancelled because of the death of his fourth wife, but we remained in touch. Edgar called me on occasion to invite me to work on this or that production, but our schedules never jibed."

"I don't know how anyone arrives at the notion that David's film concept of the empty city was a major departure from John-Michael's original stage concept," said Edgar Lansbury. "It's true that in a theater the audience is present, but do not really become integrated until Jesus is carried out on the arms and shoulders of the cast for the Resurrection. One could argue that the intermission with wine, etc. is a violation of that conceit. However, I think the idea of an empty city was wonderful, and made total sense in the introduction of the cast in their ordinary lives, followed by the scene in which John the Baptist comes across the Brooklyn Bridge, blows his Shofar, and gathers the group together for the Baptism. There were many debates between the creative team, the producers, and Columbia on the various directions that the film eventually took. That is the normal creative process, and I don't remember any major disagreements. Today," he continued, "I think the film holds up very well. It was totally unique in its use of New York City locations, and I think supports the feeling and sense of the story very admirably."

"The simple truth is," said Robin Lamont, "I had a blast making the film and felt honored to have been included in the cast. In theater, as an ensemble piece with all ten cast members on stage pretty much the whole time, our rehearsals was constant engagement—we experimented with bits, tried choreography, we were moving all the time. On the film set, we did some improvisation, but the time frame was limited because we always had a crew on hand that was working by the hour. And on film you have to hit marks, stay still while the cinematographer does his thing, and WAIT! Wait a long time between close-ups. I think the film was pretty good, but overall didn't capture the intimacy of what cast and audience most often felt during a live performance. However," she added, "I think it's amazing how we were able to come together as a cast, without ever having performed the show on stage with one another at the same time, to form a cohesive unit. The film may not have been the best ever, but I still hear from folks that they love watching it. Indeed, I know some fans who congregate with their families to see *Godspell* every Easter. How cool is that? So I'll never say that I believe that the show transferred well to screen, but then again, I don't really like many movie musicals."

"I guess," said Nic Greene, "in hindsight, that the film was quite unique. This was something special that happened at the tail end of the whole 60s era of idealism and counter-culture. Dad once told me about seeing the Living Theatre one time in New York; they had announced that they would levitate, and he had been a hundred-percent convinced they would! So if anyone was going to make a highly idealistic film where an idea and one man would galvanize a generation and bring about broad social change on the strength of a message—and that his film would actually do that—well, that was my Dad. He was amazingly naïve in some ways, at least by cynical twenty-first century standards, and he was very much his own universe. At the same time, I'd say I still share that kind of outlook and have the same kind of belief, though I think the work that follows to make that belief a reality is the more relevant factor. So, as easy as it might be to slate *Godspell*, to call it camp or otherwise, this was really a brave but failed essay toward bringing about a higher more enlightened society. I think I may not be the only one who has moved forward in life with that kind of view, it wouldn't surprise me to know that many involved with that production felt the same way."

Schwartz's original fear about the movie, the fact that it was being released so quickly after first taking hold might force the show to close early, couldn't have been farther from what actually happened. The show continued to run at the Promenade, then moved to Broadway at long last on June 22, 1976 at the Broadhurst Theater and with a cast that featured none other than Robin Lamont and David Haskell. "David and I had a very unique and special distinction," said Lamont, "because we were the only two people in the world who did the original Carnegie-Mellon production, the original LaMama production, the original Off-Broadway production, the film, and then the original Broadway production." Also in the first Broadway cast were a very happy Lamar Alford, and Toronto veteran Don Scardino, along with Elizabeth Lathram, who had been Peggy Gordon's understudy. And the show was musically directed, of all people, by Paul Shaffer, who had realized his dream of moving to New York, to conduct the band of *Saturday Night Live*. Sonia Manzano also came into the Broadway company for a short spell. After three months, the show relocated to the Plymouth Theater, then moved again in January to the Ambassador, where it would live out the remainder of its long and joyous run. When the curtain came down for the final time, on September 4th, 1977, *Godspell* had played over five hundred Broadway performances, and over two thousand Off-Broadway since the original opening night at the Cherry Lane.

Scardino also directed the first Off-Broadway revival of the show at the Lamb's Theater in 1988, which featured such powerhouses of musical theater as Eddie Korbich, Laura Dean and Trini Alvarado as well as musical direction by Doug Besterman, and had a respectable run of over two hundred shows. A second revival, at the York Theater in August of 2000 for a three-month limited run and directed by Shawn Rozsa, was much more critically acclaimed, starring such future Broadway stars as Capathia Jenkins, Chad Kimball, Leslie Kritzer, Shoshana Bean, Barrett Foa, and Eliseo Roman. In 2008, following a revival at New Jersey's famed Paper Mill Playhouse, there was talk of *Godspell* returning to Broadway at the Ethel Barrymore Theater, co-starring Gavin Creel and Diana DeGarmo, but this was not to be.

Finally, in 2011, producer Ken Davenport had the idea to bring the show back to Broadway, financed by a group called The People of *Godspell*, who each pledged a thousand dollars to own a share of the show, to run at the Circle in the Square Theater, starring Hunter Parrish and directed by Danny Goldstein. Since we do live in a time when it's once again common cultural practice to turn Broadway musicals into movies (as opposed to the trend of turning popular non-musical movies into Broadway musicals), would the cast and creators ever speculate about who might be in the remake of the film, if not the Broadway cast? "Whether stars or newcomers," said Jonas, "they would have to be great actors who stay true to the book." Lamont said, "Personally, I think it would be nutty to try and re-create the film. A new stage production is a different story. But who knows?" "As a former actor, although I don't know if anyone who's ever been actor can ever truly be 'former,' I'll always want actors to have the opportunity to work," said Hanley. "If another *Godspell* film were to be made, then that's terrific. Actors will work, and have the added bonus of enjoying the *Godspell* experience. But I do think, as I've said, that the show casts its best spell on a small stage. And it goes without saying that to use huge stars in the film might be a big mistake; talk about drawing focus!" Sammy Bayes added, "*Godspell* is an ensemble piece. If there were a need for casting the movie with name actors, I would say to be sure that the casting is brilliant." "What I think, really, is that the *Godspell* film demonstrates that movies are different animals than stage shows, and one needs to do what is best for each medium," said Stephen Schwartz. "The stage performers might or might not be the best choices for a film version, either for artistic reasons or commercial ones. I think it's hard to discuss these things theoretically, because it really comes down to specific cases."

Life, as with all things, must one day come to an end for all of us, and *Godspell*, both the original show and the film, has had its share of physical losses. The first of these just happened to have been the show's creator, John-Michael Tebelak, who succumbed to a fatal heart attack on April 2, 1985, barely thirty-five years of age. "I think what touched me the most about his death was the thought of all the unrealized dreams that died with him," said McCormick, "thoughts and ideas that he expressed often over the years; his head was always brimming with ideas. I often wonder what kind of things he would have written about had he lived. He often talked about *Godspell* as being the first part in a trilogy; wouldn't that have been something? He was a brilliant, kind, joyful, magical man. I will always be grateful to him for the faith he had in me over many years, not only as a performer but as a friend. He will always be loved and missed." Hanley recalled, "I was invited to his loft for a party shortly before the film began, and was blown away by the basketball-court-sized room where gigantic oil paintings hung. In the living room he had two turntables raised above the food, with the same record album playing (at the same time) on each. Not a big surprise that he was a playful genius!" Robert Patrick, the playwright who had been there at LaMama at the beginning and had become very close with Tebelak over the years, once said, "John-Michael told me he was embarrassed for *Godspell* to be his first show in New York. He said, 'It's just *Tom Paine* with different words.'" (*Tom Paine*, for those unfamiliar, was director Tom O'Horgan's first masterpiece for LaMama, written by Paul Foster and dazzlingly developed in workshops provided by Ellen Stewart, who found means to tour it around the United States. As she frequently put it in private conversations, "Ever since then, other little *Tom Paines* keep coming to LaMama from all over the world").

Jeffrey Mylett lost the battle with AIDS on May 7, 1986, a month shy of turning thirty-seven. McCormick recalled, "Jeff was a beloved friend. He was a devoted follower of Meher Baba, which manifested itself in a gentle nature, good humor, a little mischief and a wonderful, insatiable curiosity. He was our daughter, Eve's, godfather. His sudden passing was devastating in so many ways, not the least of which that he was so very young. We all took it extremely hard and he will always be missed." "Whenever there was a waiting period on the set, which was very often," recalled Lamont, "Jeff kept everyone entertained. He was so mischievous and playful, and he could never sit still for very long. He'd start some game or other, he'd chat with passersby, he'd make us laugh. He was always in the center of things." "At the end of our day filming 'Alas for You,'" said Hanley, "Jeff and I sat for two hours on the pier and had an amazing talk about spirituality. And the last time I spent time with him, we were both auditioning for the Los Angeles production of the Charles Schulz musical *Snoopy*. We met to spend a quick lunch together, and I'm so grateful that we did. Sadly, he wasn't cast. I would have loved to have done the show with him. His talent was amazing. He had a unique, pure style of acting, and painted emotions without words. Charlie Chaplin would have been a huge fan. I was honored to have been asked by Gilmer to sing "By My Side" at his memorial service." "Jeff and I were spiritual brothers," said Stephen Reinhardt, "me a Christian and he a disciple of the Indian mystic Meher Baba. We were both theological wannabes. We had some lively discussions about religion while strolling in the fields of Ridgefield, Connecticut, where, along with Steve Schwartz, we lived, with John-Michael not too far away. I loved these exchanges. Gilmer and I continued to spend time with him when he moved to West Hollywood, until his death. I'll never forget my last visit with him; I asked him if he was ready to move on. He nodded and pointed up, and made a flying away gesture. Death, for us both, was just an open door to another dimension."

Joseph Beruh would lose a battle with pancreatic cancer when he was sixty-five, on October 30, 1989. After *Godspell*, he and Edgar

Lansbury would go onto produce no less than six more hit shows together, among them the London revival of *Gypsy* starring Angela Lansbury and the later long-running Stephen Schwartz hit, *The Magic Show*, besides *The Night That Made America Famous* and *American Buffalo*. For the big screen, he served as executive producer for such marginal hits as *The Wild Party, Blue Sunshine*, and the horror flick *He Knows You're Alone*, which also featured Robin Lamont in a small role. "All I can say is that he was a very, very nice man and a pleasure to work with," remembered Alan Heim. "What I felt about Joe, and it was the same way I felt about Edgar and Ken Utt as well," said Hanley, "is that they all seemed like parental babysitters at the time in the very best way possible, overseeing, and holding it all together for all of us. Like how 'grownups' seem when they're forty-ish to our twenty-somethings. They smiled patiently as we skipped around in our rompers and painted faces, coming up with an improvisational day's work. That was my young take on them at the time. I also have to shyly add that I think Edgar was the most handsome thing I'd ever seen. Not to mention seeing a bit of his sister, who is my idol, in his face. Thrilling!"

Sweet, softspoken Merrell Jackson would pass at age thirty-eight on February 23, 1991, of an unknown cause. Indeed, extremely little is known about him at all, and there's quite a bit of speculation. It is known that prior to *Godspell* his following was most largely centered in the Chicago theater scene. It is also known that he never appeared in another major motion picture, or if he did, it wasn't a credited role. Some sources claim that he moved to New York once *Godspell* had finished filming, and also that he appeared in the dance ensembles of such Broadway musicals as *The Wiz* as well as on tour with Nell Carter in *Don't Bother Me, I Can't Cope*, but no online database listing exists to prove this. "The only way I can think of to describe Merrell," Hanley said, "is that he was a slender, gentle creature, and as an actor he was generously brave in his transparency. He never forced his presence in the midst of the group, but with one roll of his warm, expressive eyes, one couldn't focus on anything or anyone else. When I think about dear Merrell, I think of a modest, unselfish, and exquisitely fragile person, like valuable, fine china." McCormick added, "I just wish I could have gotten to know him better, and I think we all feel that way. He was such a sweet young man, so gentle and polite and easy to work with, but I don't recall any of us becoming close with him. Maybe Jeffrey was, but I can't remember."

The cause of Lamar Alford's demise, on April 4, 1991 at the age of forty-seven, has never been disclosed publicly. Peggy Gordon said, "Lamar's death was extremely painful, because I found out after the fact; he'd gone back to school at Morehouse College, where he then became a teacher and mentor to many other artists. It's so hard to know that I didn't have the chance to say goodbye to him." "Oh, what a big, old kindly bear he was," said McCormick. "A blend of child and man, in a Baby Huey body with a heavenly voice. For someone so big, he was able to move around the stage with such agility and lightness that it was truly surprising. He was very much loved, and his loss, again, was a huge blow. Lamar sang at our wedding, and that's the way I'll always remember him; that and his silly clown face."

Kenneth Utt, *Godspell*'s intrepid associate producer, died of natural causes at age seventy-two on January 19, 1994. He seemed never to be without a job in the movies, either as production manager, associate producer or executive producer, and the long list of impressive post-*Godspell* credits under his belt include *All That Jazz, Still of the Night, Star '80, Heaven Help Us, Something Wild, Married to the Mob, Miami Blues, Gladiator, The Silence of the Lambs,* and *Philadelphia.* He will always be remembered as extremely easygoing in the face of unthinkable pressure, and the first to smile in the face of adversity. McCormick said, "Ken was a great gentleman and a consummate professional. He was a steady hand on the set and always conducted business with a great sense of humor and kindness." Alan Heim, who came to *Godspell* in the first place after he and Utt worked together on *Liza with a Z*, said, "Kenny was always a pleasure in every sense of the word. I was very lucky to have worked with him many, many times over the years that followed, and each experience was even more terrific than the one before. It's wonderful that he'll always live on in the documentary film that Jonathan Demme made about him, *The Uttmost.*"

David Haskell would lose a battle with brain cancer on August 30, 2000, aged fifty-two. Most of his castmates, from all productions of the show as well as the film, were at his bedside for the final moments. Regrettably, his beloved wife Jeannie, with whom he fell in love at first sight when they did the show together at the Mark Taper Forum all those years earlier, lost her own battle with cancer in 2009. While he was alive, and although he never achieved the stardom his classmates at CMU were certain would one day be his, he enjoyed a career of which any actor would be proud, including television appearances on *Mary Tyler Moore, Lou Grant, Mork & Mindy* and *Falcon Crest*, transitioning smoothly between comedy and drama. He also enjoyed recurring roles on the daytime drama *Santa Barbara* and the primetime serial *Knots Landing*, and returned to the big screen in films as varied as *Body Double* and *K-9*. "There is nothing to say about David," said Lamont, "and yet everything to say. From the first day I ever met him on campus, he was simply dynamite. I think anyone who ever knew him was richer for the experience, and even more so if they got to work with him." "We spent much time in Los Angeles with David and with Jeannie, his wife, now both gone," said Reinhardt. "They arrived before us, but we eventually all joined the same church. I was the last to join, and we started to introduce the *Godspell* music to one of the services that had no music up to that point. This was the beginning of a long and close relationship for us. Our children grew up together, and often we would go over to their house after church and have brunch, and sit for hours and schmooze. His brain tumor was a sudden and tragic jolt to us all, but he was strong, and he survived, only to succumb about a year later; I'm not sure of the time period. We were with him in the hospital on his last day, and Gilmer was there when he passed. I don't know if it was that day, or another day during that week, but the tumor had left him with dementia so he thought we were all there for a meeting and asked for a yellow pad and pencil, so he could take notes. We humored him, smiling through our tears at the fragility of the human mind."

It was a shock for her *Godspell* family, as well as her tremendous worldwide legion of fans, to learn that Lynne Thigpen died very suddenly of a cerebral hemorrhage on March 12, 2003, at the age of fifty-four and at a time when she was at the top of her professional game, continuing to portray Chief on the children's geography game show, *Where in the World is Carmen Sandiego?* and the regular role of Ella Farmer on *The District*. Thigpen had spent the remainder of the 1970s post-*Godspell* appearing regularly in Broadway musicals (including *Working*, for which Stephen Schwartz was also a contributor) and made a notable appearance on the big screen in *The Warriors* in 1979, then another in *Tootsie* in 1982. By 1985 she was playing the recurring role of Nell Carter's sister Loretta on *Gimme a Break*, and in 1989 cemented herself as a dramatic powerhouse when she co-starred with Morgan Freeman in *Lean on Me*. Even while continuing her stints on *Sandiego* and *The District*, Thigpen would occasionally turn up on *All My Children* as Aunt Grace, and in such big screen projects as the futuristic Robin Williams film *Bicentennial Man*, where she portrayed the President. "Dear Lynne," said Reinhardt, "our closest friend, along with her partner, Larry, in all the years after *Godspell*. Here's a very funny story: Gilmer and I were both working shows, she doing *Godspell* and me doing *The Magic Show*. She would finish early, and head to Lynne and Larry's loft, and wait for me there to pick her up to drive back home to Ridgefield. One night I got in the car, drove home, and walked into a dark and empty house. I had no idea where Gilmer could be, and then it hit me like a brick that I had left her in New York. I'll never forget the phone call I made, the worry in Gilmer's voice when she asked where I was, and the disbelief that I left her in the city. I got right back in the car, drove the fifty-five miles again, and picked her up. Lynne, Larry and Gilmer reveled in retelling that story for years. Lynne and Larry were the only couple who had been together longer than we had, and she was like a big sister to Gilmer. She lived in New York, but whenever she came to Los Angeles, we'd get together and have a blast. It was such fun being with her. She had unlimited energy. Such a wonderful time it was when she was filming *The District*, when we were able to spend much time with her. One of our favorite things was 'Bad Movie Night,' where we'd take turns being sent out to video stores hunting for a great bad movie—movies that were so bad they were brilliant. We laughed until it hurt, and beyond. One year, she spent Halloween with us. We all dressed up, and Lynne would do her Jamaican Voodoo thing with all the kids who came into the house. She'd sit at the end of a long table with candles all over it, and the kids would be mesmerized. Such fun times. How terribly we miss her. I'll never forget that call at five in the morning from Larry. It took us a long time to come to terms with the inexplicable suddenness, and a long time to heal from losing her." "Lynne once told me that before becoming an actress, she thought she would become a nun," said Hanley. "I have no idea if she was serious, Gilmer might know, but I think Lynne might have actually started to prepare to become a nun at one point. *Thank God* for all of us that she chose a different path. Lynne was fun-loving, and had the most contagious laugh I've ever heard. She was a leader and, had we ever voted, would have been class president of the clowns. She had royal bearing and grace, and vocal cords of steel. Beyond a tragic loss!" "I think sudden death is probably the worst," said Gordon, "because it's like an amputation without anesthesia. At least with an illness, there's time to prepare for the loss, but Lynne's death was sudden and very hard."

David Greene also fell victim to pancreatic cancer on April 7, 2003, at the age of eighty-two. While he had big-screen directorial success with such movies as 1978's *Gray Lady Down, London Conspiracy* in 1980 and *Hard Country* the following year, the remainder of his career was most largely spent at the directorial helm of television dramas, including the iconic *Roots* in 1977. After losing fourth wife Thomasina while *Godspell* was opening across the globe (mother of his second son, Laurence), he married fifth wife Vanessa in 1975 and fathered third son Linsel, by all accounts as much a character as his father was. Sixth wife Lauren, whom he married eight days after his divorce from Vanessa and whom he would divorce in 1981, became son Laurence's adoptive mother. He married his seventh and final wife, Kelly, three days before his passing.

Surviving members of the cast and crew have all led interesting lives since that time, with varying degrees of success both in and out of the entertainment sector. Peggy Gordon has seen "By My Side" performed and recorded countless times, most recently and notably by pop icon Tori Amos. She herself has never lacked for work as a vocalist for recording sessions, also enjoyed employment in several daytime dramas, and became one of the most in-demand writers in New York City.

Nearly four decades after leaving *Godspell* for her very first episode of *Sesame Street*, Sonia Manzano is still a treasured international star of educational programming in her role of Maria. She also guest-starred in a notable two-part episode of *BJ and the Bear* in 1979, and more recently embodied a strong supporting role in the 2005 big screen comedy *Dumped!* In addition, she's begun writing a series of children's books for Scholastic.

Nina Faso has arguably directed more productions of *Godspell* than any other individual in the show's history. She left the business of show of her own volition and moved to San Diego with beloved husband Richard, where the two run a business in the fields of finance and real estate.

Herb Braha continued to work as an actor until the mid 1990s, making appearances on such television dramas as *Kojak* and *Remington Steele*, and made a last big screen appearance in the cult favorite *Child's Play 2*. He has since crossed over to work behind the scenes, running a business in California that supplies fabric for theatrical and film costumes.

Stephen Nathan enjoys tremendous success today in many different facets of television. He continued acting until the mid 1980s, notably portraying a regular role on the short-lived but popular sitcom *Busting Loose* with Adam Arkin and Barbara Rhoades, but had already begun flexing his muscles as a writer for episodes of *Laverne and Shirley* among others, later becoming the head writer for such series as *Joan of Arcadia* and *Bones* as well as serving as executive producer or consulting producer for episodes of both. More recently, and in a return to work in film after a long absence, he was the creative consultant for the 2011 comedy *The Oranges*, starring Oliver Platt, Alison Janney and Catherine Keener. He did return to the role of Jesus a final time in 1985, when he and David Haskell performed "All for the Best" on the PBS presentation *The Best of Broadway*, hosted by Tom Bosley and coordinated by Lee Becker Theodore of the American Dance Machine.

Joanne Jonas initially remained an extremely committed actress, and in 1975 made an appearance on Broadway as Letta in the revival of Arthur Miller's *Death of a Salesman*, starring George C. Scott along with Teresa Wright, James Farentino, Harvey Keitel and Craig Wasson. But growing weary of life on the boards, she completely quit in 1977 and moved to California with her husband and son to begin a more anonymous existence. Today, under her new name of JJ McCraty, she very happily works as the Director of Desktop Publishing for HeartMath, a company committed to stress-reduction programs through mathematical applications. Widespread rumors circulated for years that she had obtained a law degree and become a high-powered theatrical agent in New York City, but no one knows the source or why they began.

Gilmer McCormick continued a long and distinguished acting career on screens big and small, in such films as *Starting Over* with Jill Clayburgh and in episodes of *Hill Street Blues*, as well as the made-for-TV movie *The Burning Bed* with Farrah Fawcett. In 2003 she began teaching at the Young Actors Space in Sherman Oaks and was ultimately promoted to co-director in 2007, but has since re-relocated to her native Kentucky, where she enjoys involvement with the Actor's Theater of Louisville. She is still very happily married to Stephen Reinhardt, and in 2011 the couple welcomed the birth of their first grandchild. Reinhardt, meanwhile, still enjoys work as a musical director, most largely in the field of daytime drama, where he has supervised the scoring of *General Hospital* and *Days of our Lives*, among many others.

Robin Lamont eventually starred on Broadway as Sandy in *Grease* and also in the original company of *Working* (alongside Lynne Thigpen), as well as work in such films as *He Knows You're Alone* and a recurring role on *Ryan's Hope*. Several years ago she opted for a completely new career path, returning to school for her law degree and ultimately becoming an Assistant District Attorney in Westchester County, where she lives with husband Ken and raised her sons. More recently, she switched gears again and has embarked on a career as a suspense novelist, making her debut with the critically-acclaimed crime drama *If Thy Right Hand*, pressed by Dog Ear Publishing.

Katie Hanley continued to enjoy success as an actress in such films as *Xanadu* and as a guest star on *Charlie's Angels*, but has completely left entertainment altogether. She is very happy to be a wife and mother all but removed from the public eye, and enjoys sculpting as a hobby and passion.

Jerry Sroka lives in Southern California with wife Mariette Hartley, and considers his other two proudest achievements to be daughter Liz and son Warren. In 1980 he began a long and successful career as a voice-over artist, most recently for the animated series *The Life and Times of Tim*, but has also stayed in front of the lens on episodes of *Seinfeld, Ellen, Murphy Brown, Ally McBeal* and *The Practice*. In 2011 he made an appearance on a popular episode of the Showtime series *Shameless*, starring William H. Macy and Emmy Rossum.

Alan Heim has barely ever gone a day before or since *Godspell* without employment as a highly-demanded editor for film and television. Aside from winning the Oscar for *All That Jazz* as well as a BAFTA Award and the American Cinema Editors Award, he had been previously nominated for an Oscar for *Network*. His other film achievements include *Lenny, Hair, Valmont, Copycat, The Adventures of Pluto Nash* and *The Notebook*. For television, aside from his Emmy nomination for *Liza with a Z*, he worked on *Holocaust* and won additional awards for both *Introducing Dorothy Dandridge* and *Grey Gardens*. In 2006, he served as President of the American Cinema Editors.

Nic Greene also embarked on a career path in entertainment, initially as an actor, but not because of his father David. "He was very discouraging of me acting. At one point I was going to go to Cal Arts to study filmmaking, but didn't. I think he wouldn't have minded that so much. He was pretty opinionated, and didn't have much awareness of how his views might or might not impact another. At the same time, I'm sure that having a father who worked in the film business, was a patron of the arts and music and was really pretty open-minded when it came to creativity, had quite a lot to do with my having worked creatively for the bulk of my life. When it comes down to it he was a self-made man, he had worked up from being the son of a Bethnal Green barber to being a highly-respected and always-working director, so he was in his rights to be tough." In any case, he worked steadily as a character actor for ten years beginning in 1990, most notably on an episode of *The Nanny* with Fran Drescher, as a video director working on 'The Bobbi Flekman Story,' a way of capitalizing on the character Drescher so notably portrayed in the film *This is Spinal Tap!* He switched gears soon after the turn of the century and became a retoucher for photographs and entertainment posters, for such films as *The Matrix* and *Money Train*, and *A Bright Shining Lie* for HBO Original Films, besides such television projects as *The Dog Whisperer*.

Sammy Bayes, also known professionally as Sammy Dallas Bayes, continued choreography and musical staging on Broadway for such musicals as *Shelter* and *Rainbow Jones*, and once again took to the stage in *Fiddler on the Roof* in the show's 1976 revival, starring Zero Mostel. In 1983 he choreographed Stephen Schwartz's *The Magic Show* for Canadian television, then returned to New York to assist with choreographic reconstruction for both *Jerome Robbins' Broadway* and the 1990 revival of *Fiddler on the Roof*, starring Topol, Marcia Lewis and Ruth Jaroslow. Since that time, he has repaired to the upstate New York city of Oneonta, where he has become the director-in-residence for the Orpheum Theater there, helming such productions as *Oliver!, Footloose, Phantom of the Opera*, and *A Funny Thing Happened on the Way to the Forum*. He continues to enjoy a long and happy marriage with wife Barbara, and couldn't be more proud of son Taylor or daughter Alexa.

Edgar Lansbury continued producing in all media very successfully, including involvement in the 2011 Broadway revival of *Godspell*. In 1987 he produced the made-for-TV thriller *A Stranger Waits*, starring Suzanne Pleshette, and in 1999 was the force behind the big screen comedy-drama *Advice from a Caterpillar*, with Cynthia Nixon, Timothy Olyphant and Andy Dick.

Since *Godspell*, Victor Garber has become one of the greatest stars of his generation, whether on stage or screen. In 1973 he won the Theatre World Award for his Off-Broadway appearance in Henrik Ibsen's *Ghosts*. After a few television appearances and a supporting role in the Canadian film *Monkeys in the Attic* in 1974, he came into his own as a theater legend when he created the role of Cliff Anderson in Ira Levin's *Deathtrap*, for which he received a Tony nomination and which was later portrayed on screen by Christopher Reeve. After replacing Tony Roberts in *They're Playing Our Song* (who had in turn replaced Robert Klein in the original production), he created the role of Anthony in *Sweeney Todd* to tremendous acclaim, then switched back to non-musical craft in the original cast of *Noises Off*, for which he received a Drama Desk Award. In 1985, he took on the starring role of Jackson Beaudine in the television series *I Had Three Wives*, and was even once again directed by David Greene in 1988 when he played the title role in *Liberace: Behind the Music*. He returned to Broadway with *Lend Me a Tenor* in 1989 and garnered another Tony nomination in the process, then in 1993 embodied the strong supporting role of Greg on film in *Sleepless in Seattle*. His final Tony nomination to date came a year later, when he starred as Applegate in the revival of *Damn Yankees*, and his name became a household word in 1997 when he portrayed Thomas Andrews in the smash hit movie *Titanic*. 1998 found him creating the role of Serge in *Art* on Broadway opposite Alan Alda and Alfred Molina, and from 2001 through 2006 he became a popular regular attraction on the TV series *Alias* as Jack, the father of Sydney Bristow as played by Jennifer Garner. More recently, he enjoyed success on the series *Eli Stone* as well as Lisa Kudrow's cable series *Web Therapy*, and in 2011 became the voice of boss Charles Townsend on the newfangled version of *Charlie's Angels*.

Just as *Godspell* was in the throes of post-production, Stephen Schwartz saw the Broadway launch of his beloved *Pippin* at the Imperial Theater, with a cast starring Ben Vereen, John Rubinstein, Jill Clayburgh, Leland Palmer, Irene Ryan, and a chorus that included a then-unknown Ann Reinking as its featured dancer. The show would run for five years and mark another international smash, and Schwartz received two Tony nominations for it. 1974 would give way to *The Magic Show* starring Doug Henning, and then *Working* opened in 1978, which won a Drama Desk Award and received two Tony nominations, besides the two Schwartz received when *Godspell* transferred to Broadway. Schwartz would also direct *Working* four years later as a production for *American Playhouse* on PBS starring, among others, Eileen Brennan, Rita Moreno, Patti LaBelle, Barbara Hershey, Barbara Barrie, Didi Conn, Barry Bostwick, Charles Haid and Scatman Crothers, and was hosted by Studs Terkel. In 1986 his musical *Rags* was produced at the Mark Hellinger starring Teresa Stratas and Larry Kert, and although the Broadway community had the highest possible hopes for the show (and Schwartz received another Tony nomination for it), it flopped resoundingly. In the mid-1990s, Schwartz supplied the lyrics to the popular animated Disney film *Pocahontas* with music by Alan Menken (which won two Oscars for Schwartz's contributions), and then the full score to the equally-acclaimed *The Hunchback of Notre Dame*, as well as the song "When You Believe" to *The Prince of Egypt* (which won another Oscar). 2003 found the latest in his long line of international hits, namely *Wicked*, which won a Drama Desk Award and received two Tony nominations. But *Godspell* remains the only Stephen Schwartz musical to have ever received a big screen treatment in live action.

When all is said and done and in the final analysis, Peggy Gordon perhaps summed it up the most clearly, most dearly and most nearly. "If you read David Greene's Wikipedia biography, he states that although he and John-Michael began collaborating on the screenplay, it really wound up being all David Greene because it veered away from John-Michael's concept of an empty world, and focused instead on a world empty of people. Now, did this work? Yeah. It did. Somehow, the emotional power of the show did in fact translate in the juxtaposition David created. Millions of fans have come to *Godspell* through stock and amateur productions, but millions have also come though the movie, and have been as moved as those audience members who've seen it live."

Ergo, as guessed, it was all for the best.

THE END

INDEX

1776, 31, 45
41st Street Theater, 25
A&R Studios, 49
Academy Awards (Oscars), 24, 145, 147
Achziger, Lowell, 18-19
Actor's Theater of Louisville, 144
Adventures of Pluto Nash, The, 145
Advice from a Caterpillar, 146
"Alas for You," 13, 29, 50, 109, 137
Albertson, Jack, 24
Alda, Alan, 147
Alford, Lamar, 28-29, 31-32, 44, 48, 108, 134, 139
Alias, 147
"All for the Best," 28-29, 50, 82, 87, 102-103, 105-106, 118, 127, 143
"All Good Gifts," 29, 44, 108
All My Children, 141
All That Jazz, 139, 145
Ally McBeal, 145
Alvarado, Trini, 135
Amazon, 124
Ambassador Theater, 24, 135
American Academy of Dramatic Arts, 27
American Buffalo, 138
American Cinema Editors, 145
American Dance Machine, 143
American Graffiti, 124
American Playhouse, 147

American Street Theater, 18, 129
Amos, Tori, 142
Andrews, Julie, 39
Annie Get Your Gun, 39
Ari, Bob, 18-19, 55, 63
Arkin, Adam, 143
Arnold, Ginger, 3
Arnold, Janet S., 4
Arnold, Ken, 4
Art, 147
BAFTA Awards, 145
Bandshell, Central Park, 107
"Baptism," 12, 83, 93-94, 96-97, 101, 133
Barnes, Clive, 17
Barrie, Barbara, 147
Barry Sisters, 4
Baum, Rebecca, 32
Bayes, Alexa, 146
Bayes, Barbara, 146
Bayes, Sammy (Sammy Dallas Bayes), 8, 38, 40, 95-99, 103, 107, 128-129, 132, 136, 146
Bayes, Taylor, 146
Bean, Shoshana, 135
Beatles, The, 50
"Beautiful City," 52-53, 110, 126
Beck, Julian, 19
Beckett, Samuel, 25
Beef and Ale, The, 43
Bergman, Ingrid, 113

Beruh, Joseph, 13-14, 23-24, 26, 33, 35-36, 40, 43, 53, 123, 137-38
Best of Broadway, The, 143
Besterman, Doug, 135
Bethesda Fountain, 83, 94, 96-97, 110
"Betrayal by Judas," 30, 112
Bicentennial Man, 141
Billboard Top 100, 34
BJ and the Bear, 142
Blake, Kathleen, 36
"Bless the Lord," 11, 29, 41-42, 47, 68, 107
Bloomingdale's, 42
Blue Sunshine, 138
Blume, Bobby, 6
Bock, Jerry, 27
Body Double, 140
Bogarde, Dirk, 36
Bolick, Duane, 18, 20, 22, 26
Bones, 143
Bosley, Tom, 143
Bostwick, Barry, 147
Braha, Herb, 12, 20, 29, 31-33, 43, 107, 143
Brecht, Bertholt, 24
Brel, Jacques, 4
Bremseth, Lloyd, 43
Brennan, Eileen, 147
Bright Shining Lie, A, 145
Broadhurst Theater, 134
Broadway Arts, 95
Bruch, Max, 5
Bulova-Accutron sign, 103, 105, 118, 127
Burnett, Carol, 39
Burning Bed, The, 144
Busting Loose, 143
"By My Side," 7, 22, 26, 29, 31, 52, 110, 122, 131, 137, 142
Byrd, David, 31
Caffe Cino, 19
Callan, Michael, 7
Canada, Jimmy, 20, 27
Canby, Vincent, 117
Cannes Film Festival, 91, 123
Cannon, Freddie 'Boom-Boom', 4
Canterbury Tales, The, 38
Carmina Burana, 4
Carnegie Mansion, 103
Carnegie-Mellon University (CMU), 18-20, 22, 25, 29, 31-33, 45, 55-66, 134, 140
Carr, Norman, 50
Carson, Johnny, 45
Carter, Nell, 138, 141
Cassidy, David, 43
CBS, 24, 35
Central Park, 75-77, 94-95, 97, 101-102, 107-109, 120
Channing, Carol, 39
Chaplin, Charlie, 137
Charles DeGaulle Airport, 91
Charlie's Angels, 144, 147
Cheetah, The, 13
Chelsea Piers, 88, 109
Cherry Lane Theater, 17, 24, 28-29, 39, 44, 49, 52, 109-110, 135
Chicago Sun-Times, 119
Child's Play 2, 143
Children's Television Workshop, 41
Chinatown, 20
Circle in the Square Theater, 7
Clayburgh, Jill, 144, 147
Climax, 35
Clooney, Rosemary, 4
Coasters, The, 4
Columbia Pictures, 35-36, 40, 43, 93, 95, 113, 123, 133
Commedia Dell'Arte, 18
Compulsion, 24
Conn, Didi, 147
Copycat, 145
Coronet Blue, 24, 36-37
Covington, Julie, 45
Coward, Noel, 4

Creel, Gavin, 135
Cries and Whispers, 124
Croisette, 123
Crothers, Scatman, 147
"Crucifixion," 17, 30, 112
Cutler, Jesse, 13, 28
Damn Yankees, 147
Danny and the Juniors, 4
Danson, Randy, 18-19, 55, 57
Dark Light, The, 36
Daughter of Darkness, 36
Davenport, Ken, 135
David Frost Show, The, 67-68
Davis, Bette, 131-132
"Day by Day," 6, 17, 28-31, 34-35, 40, 50-51, 53, 67, 78, 85, 101-102, 113, 118, 122, 131
Day, Doris, 4
Days of Our Lives, 144
Dean, Laura, 135
Death of a Salesman, 143
Deathtrap, 146
Defenders, The, 24, 37
deGarmo, Diana, 135
Demme, Jonathan, 139
Denham, Reginald, 24
DeNiro, Robert, 23
Devins, George, 50
Dick, Andy, 146
District, The, 140-141
Dog Ear Publishing, 144
Dog Whisperer, The, 145
Don't Bother Me, I Can't Cope, 138
Drama Desk Awards, 33, 146-148
Drescher, Fran, 145
Drifters, The, 4
Dumped!, 143
Duncan, Stuart, 13, 25, 35
Duplex, The, 7
Dynasty, 12
East River, 79, 104, 111-112
Eatwell, Brian, 37

Ebert, Roger, 119
Ebb, Fred, 27
Eli Stone, 147
Ellen, 145
Elsa Lanchester, Herself, 25
Emmy Awards, 145
Empire Diner, 94
Essex, David, 35, 45, 100
Ethel Barrymore Theater, 135
Exorcist, The, 124
Falcon Crest, 140
FAO Schwarz, 94
Farentino, James, 143
Fargue, Annie, 35
Faso, Nina, 7-8, 18, 20-21, 25, 30, 33, 38, 125, 143
Fawcett, Farrah, 144
Fiddler on the Roof, 5, 38, 146
Fitzgerald, Ella, 5
Fitzstephens, Jack, 98
Foa, Barrett, 135
Footloose, 146
Fordham University, 102
Forella, Michael, 32, 67-69
Forest Hills Stadium, 5
Forster, John, 7
Fosse, Bob, 37
Foster, Paul, 136
Four Lads, The, 4
Freeman, Morgan, 141
Funny Thing Happened on the Way to the Forum, A, 146
Ganapoler, Paul, 37
Garber, Victor, 8, 12, 34, 45-48, 52-53, 72, 79, 87, 91-92, 95, 100, 103, 110-111, 113-114, 118, 121, 123, 127, 130, 146
Garfunkel, Art, 4
Garner, Jennifer, 147
Gaslight, 24
Gaynor, Mitzi, 39
General Hospital, 144
Ghosts, 146

Gilda Radner: Live from New York, 12
Gimme a Break, 141
Gladiator, 136
Godfrey, John, 37, 102
Godspell Drinking Game, 125
Godspell Four, The, 29-30, 50
Gold, Andrew, 4
Goldblatt, Phil, 38
Golden Madonna, The, 36
Goldstein, Danny, 135
Goodyear Playhouse, 36
Gordon, Peggy, 7, 19, 22, 26, 28-29, 31-34, 40-42, 114, 122, 134, 139, 142, 148
Grammy Awards, 31, 34
Grand Canyon, 11
Grand Teton National Theater, 24
Grand Theater, 45
Grant's Tomb, 80, 106-107
Grappelli, Stephane, 4
Gravine, Mickey, 50
Gray Lady Down, 142
Grease, 131, 144
Greene, David, 35-49, 54, 71, 92-102, 107, 110-113, 118, 120-123, 127-133, 142-143, 145-146, 148
Greene, Kelly, 142
Greene, Lauren, 142
Greene, Laurence, 142
Greene, Linsel, 142
Greene, Nicolas, 8, 100, 134, 145
Greene, Thomasina, 142
Greene, Vanessa, 142
Grey Gardens, 146
Gypsy, 39, 138
Haid, Charles, 19, 23, 147
Hair, 5, 17, 26, 95, 145
Hale, Corky, 53
Hallmark Hall of Fame, 36
Halpern, Belle, 38, 74
Hamburger, Jay, 22
Hammerstein II, Oscar, 5

Hanley, Katie, 8, 32, 40-42, 46-48, 51, 67-70, 72-84, 86-89, 92, 94-95, 97-98, 101-103, 105, 108-114, 122-123, 125, 131, 135-138, 142, 144
Hard Country, 142
Hard Day's Night, A, 127
Harnick, Sheldon, 27
Harris, Julie, 36
Harrison, George, 50
Hartley, Mariette, 7, 144
Haskell, David, 18-19, 28-29, 31-32, 40, 42, 46, 55, 59, 75, 79, 83, 87, 91-92, 94, 96, 103, 118, 120, 123, 134, 139, 143
Haskell, Jeannie (Jeannie Lange), 32, 123, 140
Hayes, Helen, 69
He Knows You're Alone, 138
HeartMath, 143
Heaven Help Us, 139
Heifetz, Jascha, 4
Heim, Alan, 8, 37, 99, 103, 106, 109, 113, 132, 138-139, 145
Heimann, Richard, 37, 71-72, 97, 100
Heller, Randee, 32, 67-68
Hello, Dolly!, 39
Henning, Doug, 147
Henson, Jim, 41
Hepburn, Audrey, 39
Hershey, Barbara, 147
Hideout, The, 36
Hill Street Blues, 144
Hilliard, Ryan, 32, 68
Hobson, Valerie, 36
Holmes, Prudence Wright, 20, 27
Holocaust, 145
Hordern, Michael, 36
Horton, Captain, 18
Hunchback of Notre Dame, The, 147
Hutton, Betty, 39
I Can Get It For You Wholesale, 25

I Had Three Wives, 146
I Start Counting, 37
Ibsen, Henrik, 146
If Thy Right Hand, 7
IMDB, 124
Imperial Theater, 147
Intercontinental Carleton, 123
Introducing Dorothy Dandridge, 145
Irons, Jeremy, 35, 42, 45
It's a Wonderful Life, 129
Jack, Eileen Grace, 100
Jackson, Merrell, 44, 46-48, 92-93, 108-109, 138
Jacques Brel is Alive and Well and Living in Paris, 5
Jacobs, Martha, 18, 55, 62
Janney, Alison, 143
Jaroslow, Ruth, 146
Jenkins, Capathia, 135
Jerome Robbins' Broadway, 146
Jesus Christ Superstar, 14, 17, 124, 128
Joan of Arcadia, 143
John Golden Theater, 23
Jonas, Bert, 27
Jonas, Joanne (JJ McCraty), 8, 17, 27-29, 32, 34, 38, 40-41, 46-47, 67-68, 70, 79, 83, 92, 97, 99, 103, 105-109, 111, 113-114, 129-130, 135, 143
Joyce, James, 94
K-9, 140
Kadima Singers, The, 4
Kamen, Michael, 13, 50
Kander, John, 27
Kaye, Judy, 33
Kazazskow, Ben, 37
Keel, Howard, 36
Keener, Catherine, 143
Keitel, Harvey, 143
Kennedy's Children, 23
Kerr, Deborah, 39
Kert, Larry, 147

Kimball, Chad, 135
King, Stan, 18, 55, 65
King & I, The, 39
Kittiwake Island, 24
Klein, Robert, 146
Knight, Shirley, 23
Kojak, 143
Korbich, Eddie, 135
Kudrow, Lisa, 147
Kritzer, Leslie, 135
La Boheme, 4
LaBelle, Patti, 147
LaBonte, Richard, 13, 28
Laine, Frankie, 4
LaMama Experimental Theater Company, 19-23, 26, 134, 136-137
Lamb's Theater, 135
Lamont, Robin, 6-8, 18-21, 27, 29, 31-34, 40, 46, 48, 51, 55, 64, 71, 78, 80, 83, 85, 91-92, 94, 97-98, 101-103, 105, 107-109, 111-113, 118, 122-123, 125, 131, 133-135, 137-138, 140, 144
Lane, Margaret, 36
Lang, Fritz, 98
Lansbury, Angela, 24, 114, 138
Lansbury, Bruce, 23
Lansbury, Edgar, 8, 13-14, 23-26, 33, 35-37, 40-41, 43-45, 47, 53, 92, 98, 103, 109, 112-114, 121, 123, 132-133, 137-138, 146
"Last Supper," 112
Last Tango in Paris, 124
Lathram, Elizabeth, 32, 67-68, 70, 134
Laverne & Shirley, 143
Lawrence, Carol, 39
Lean on Me, 141
"Learn Your Lessons Well," 29, 52, 109,
Leave it to Jane, 24
Lehrer, Tom, 5

Lend Me a Tenor, 146
Lenny, 145
Lerner, Alan Jay, 5
Lester, Richard, 118, 127-128
Levin, Ira, 146
Levins, Daniel, 96
Levy, Eugene, 12, 33,
Lewis, Marcia, 146
Liberace: Behind the Music, 146
Life and Times of Tim, The, 144
"Light of the World," 29, 52, 79, 111, 127
Lincoln Center, 82, 86, 90, 102-103, 105, 108-111, 113-114
Living Theater, The, 19, 134
Lindstrom, Pia, 113
Liza with a Z, 37, 139, 145
Lodge, Henry Cabot, 43
Loesser, Frank, 5
Loewe, Frederick, 5
Loft Players, The, 24
London Conspiracy, 142
Look to the Lilies, 24
Lou Grant, 140
Louis and the Elephant, 25
Lubitsch, Ernst, 98
Lynley, Carol, 36
Macey, Charles, 50
MacGill, Moira, 23
MacGoohan, Patrick, 114
Macy, William H., 145
Magic Show, The, 147
Makeba, Miriam, 5
Malina, Judith, 19
Mame, 24
Manes, Steve, 50
Manilow, Barry, 4
Mantell, Robert B., 24
Manzano, Sonia, 7, 18-19, 28-29, 31-32, 34, 39-42, 47, 55, 61, 67-70, 134, 142
Mark Hellinger Theater, 147
Mark Taper Forum, 31, 33, 140

Married to the Mob, 139
Marshall, E.G., 24
Martin, Andrea, 12, 34
Martin, Mary, 39
Martin, Tony, 4
Martinique Theater, 24
Mary Tyler Moore, 140
Matrix, The, 145
Mayor's Office of Film, 49
Mayron, Melanie, 33
Mazziotti, Mary, 18, 55, 66
McAssey, Michael, 7
McCartney, Paul, 4
McCormick, Gilmer, 8, 12, 17, 19, 22, 29-34, 39-41, 46, 52, 76, 79, 81, 88, 90, 92, 97, 100, 103-104, 106-108, 110, 113-114, 121, 128, 136-142, 144
McCracken, Hugh, 50
Meher Baba, 137
Menken, Alan, 147
Merman, Ethel, 39
Meyer, Carla, 33
Miami Blues, 139
Midler, Bette, 4
Miller, Arthur, 143
Minister of Culture of France, 123
Minnelli, Liza, 37
Mitchell, Guy, 4
Molina, Alfred, 147
Money Train, 145
Monkeys in the Attic, 146
Montgomery, Barbara, 23
Moore, Dorothy, 4
Morehouse College, 139
Moreno, Rita, 39, 147
Mork & Mindy, 140
MOS, 98
Mostel, Zero, 146
Muppets, 41
Murphy Brown, 145
My Fair Lady, 39

Mylett, Jeffrey, 20-22, 29, 31-32, 34, 40, 42, 46, 52, 77, 80, 83, 92-93, 100, 105, 125, 137, 139
Nanny, The, 145
Nash Information Services, 124
Nathan, Stephen, 20, 28-31, 45, 139, 143
Network, 145
Neveu, Ginette, 4
New York Times, 17, 73, 117
Newman, Paul, 6
Night That Made America Famous, The, 138
Nixon, Cynthia, 146
Nixon, Marni, 39
Noises Off, 146
Notebook, The, 145
O'Horgan, Tom, 136
Oliver!, 146
Olivor, Jane, 7
Olyphant, Timothy, 146
"On The Willows," 29, 112
Only Game in Town, The, 24
Oranges, The, 143
Orlons, The, 4
Orpheum Theater (Oneonta, NY), 146
Oysher, Moyshe, 4
Page, Patti, 4
Palais du Festival, 123
Palmer, Leland, 147
Paper Mill Playhouse, 135
Paper Moon, 124
"Parable of the Good Samaritan," 81, 106, 125
"Parable of the Prodigal Son," 52, 109-110
"Parable of the Rich Man and Lazarus," 106-107, 121
Paper Mill Playhouse, 135
"Parable of the Sheep," 106
Parrish, Hunter, 135
Parsons, Louella, 8

Patrick, Robert, 8, 23, 45, 136
PBS, 143, 147
People of *Godspell*, The, 135
People Next Door, The, 36
Phantom of the Opera, The, 146
Pharisee Monster, 6, 13, 88, 109-110
Pharisees, 29, 123
Philadelphia, 139
Piaf, Edith, 4
Pippin, 147
Pitchford, Dean, 32, 67-69
Planner, Mark 'Binky', 32, 67-68
Platt, Oliver, 143
Playhouse 90, 35
Pleshette, Suzanne, 146
Plymouth Theater, 135
Porte St. Martin, 35
Pocahontas, 147
Porter, Cole, 5
Practice, The, 145
"Prepare Ye, the Way of the Lord," 5, 29-30, 50, 93-94, 101, 113
Preston, Billy, 50
"Prologue," 22, 93, 96, 101
Prince of Egypt, The, 147
Promenade!, 25
Promenade Theater, 25, 39, 69-70, 117
Psalms 98:4, 15
Queensborough Bridge (Edward I. Koch Bridge), 109
Quinn, Doug, 20
Quinn, Marty, 20
Quinn, Richard, 20
Rabin, Michael, 4
Radner, Gilda, 12, 34, 48,
Rags, 147
Rainbow Jones, 146
"Raven and the Swan, The," 22-23
RCA, 26-27
Red Skelton Hour, The, 24
Reed, Oliver, 36
Reed, Robert, 24

Reeve, Christopher, 146
Reinhardt, Stephen, 8, 12-13, 27-28, 30, 33, 41, 44, 50-53, 114, 121, 137, 140-141, 144
Reinking, Ann, 147
Remington Steele, 143
Rennie, Michael, 36
"Resurrection," 21, 133
Rhoades, Barbara, 143
Rivals, The, 25-26
Riverside Park, 107
Robbins, Jerome, 38
Roberts, Tony, 146
Rodgers, Richard, 5
Rohrer, Andy, 18-20, 31, 55-56, 60
Roman, Eliseo, 135
Rooney, Mickey, 15
Roots, 142
Rosoff, Elliot, 50
Ross, Diana, 4
Rosselini, Isabella, 113
Rossum, Emmy, 145
Rothschilds, The, 5
Roundhouse Theater, 35
Royal Alexandria Theater, 46
Royale Theater, 25
Rozsa, Shawn, 135
Rubinstein, John, 147
Russell, Rosalind, 39
Ryan, Irene, 147
Ryan's Hope, 144
Ryder, Amy, 7
Sacks, Michael, 23
Sagnelli, Phylliss, 38
Salvation, 17
Santa Barbara, 140
Sardi's, 17
Saturday Night Live, 12, 134
"Save the People," 29-30, 93, 97, 101, 121
Scardino, Don, 12, 134-135
Schacht, Danielle, 3
Scheiner, Eliot, 51

Schickel, Richard, 120-121
Showcase Studios, 95
Schwab's, 11
Schwartz, Stephen, 7-9, 11, 13-14, 25-27, 30-31, 33, 36, 38, 40, 44, 50-53, 94, 99-100, 103, 106, 109-110, 115, 118, 121-123, 127, 129, 134, 136-138, 141, 146-148
Scorsese, Martin, 129
Scott, Angela, 34
Scott, George C., 143
Screen Actors Guild, 49
SCTV, 12
Sebastian, 36
"Seed Parable," 84, 102
Seinfeld, 145
Sesame Street, 41-42, 142
Shaffer, Paul, 8, 11-14, 34, 50-52, 113, 134
Shameless, 145
Sheen, Martin, 24
Shelter, 146
Sheridan, Richard Brinsley, 25
Sheridan Square Theater, 24-25
Sherman, Allan, 5
Shore, Dinah, 4
Short, Martin, 12, 34, 42
Shubert Theater, 25
Shutter, Ricky, 13, 28, 30
Shuttered Room, The, 36
Silence of the Lambs, The, 139
Simon, Carly, 4
Simon, Paul, 4
Sleepless in Seattle, 147
Snoopy, 137
Something Wild, 139
Sondheim, Stephen, 5
Songs in Blume, 6
Soper, Gay, 45
Sound of Hunting, A, 24
Sound of Music, The, 39
South Pacific, 39
Sponseller, Howie, 32, 67-68

Squares, 33
Sroka, Jerry, 7-8, 33, 43, 46-48, 53, 73, 81, 92, 95, 98, 100, 104, 106, 110-111, 113-114, 124, 130, 144
Sroka, Liz, 144
Sroka, Warren, 144
Star '80, 139
Star Witness, 24
Starting Over, 144
Staton, Dakota, 4
Statue of Liberty, 111
Stevens, Jamie, 18, 55, 58
Stewart, Ellen, 19-20, 23, 136
Still of the Night, 139
Sting, The, 124
Stop the World, I Want to Get Off, 5
Strange Affair, The, 37
Stranger Waits, A, 146
Stratas, Teresa, 147
Streisand, Barbra, 4, 25
Studio One, 35
Styne, Jule, 5
Subject Was Roses, The, 24-25, 37
Sucher, Sherrie, 37, 48
Sugar Shoppe, The, 45
Sullivan, Ed, 45
Sweeney Todd, 146
Sweet Charity, 5
Tamar, Chayim, 50
Taylor, Elizabeth, 6
Tebelak, John-Michael, 8, 18-21, 28, 30, 35-36, 38-40, 73, 92, 101, 109, 118, 121-122, 129, 133, 136-137, 148
Terkel, Studs, 147
That Summer – That Fall, 24
Theater de Lys, 24
Theatre World Awards, 146
Theodore, Lee Becker, 143
They're Playing Our Song, 146
Thigpen, Lynne, 7, 32, 40-41, 46-48, 76, 79, 83, 86, 90, 92, 94, 104-105, 107-108, 132, 140-142, 144
This is Spinal Tap!, 145
Thomas, Dave, 12
Thomas, Don, 50
Thomson, Gordon, 12
Threepenny Opera, The, 24
Time magazine, 120
Titanic, 147
Tokens, The, 4
Tom Paine, 136
Tomlinson, David, 36
Tony Awards, 24, 38, 146-148
Tootsie, 141
Topol, 146
"Tower of Babel," 29
"Turn Back, O Man," 27-29, 41, 47, 103
Turner, Lana, 11
Tzu, Susan, 8, 18-19, 21, 29, 35, 55-66
Ulysses, 94
Umpire Rock, Central Park, 108
United Scenic Artists, 37
University of Toronto, 45
Ustinov, Isolde Denny, 24
Ustinov, Peter, 24
Utt, Kenneth, 37, 39, 99, 138-139
Uttmost, The, 139
Valmont, 145
Van Eyssen, John, 36, 113
Variety, 38, 124
Vereen, Ben, 44, 147
von Stroheim, Erich, 98
Waiting for Godot, 25
Wallach, Eli, 36
Ward's Island, 72-74, 78, 81, 84-85, 92, 101-102, 106, 112
Warriors, The, 141
Wasson, Craig, 143
Way of Life, A, 24
Way We Were, The, 124
"We Beseech Thee," 29, 52, 110,

Web Therapy, 147
Webb, Marti, 45
Weill, Kurt, 24
West, Mae, 99, 106
West Side Story, 39
Westbury Music Fair, 7
"When You Believe," 147
Where in the World is Carmen Sandiego?, 140-141
Wicked, 148
Wilbur Theater, 43
Wild Party, The, 138
Williams, Robin, 141
Winter Garden Theater, 12
Wiz, The, 138
WNEW-TV, 5
Wolf, Hope, 45
Wolf's Deli, 13

Wordpress.com, 7
Working, 141, 145, 147
World Trade Center (Twin Towers), 89, 104-106, 119
Wood, Natalie, 39
Wooden Horse, The, 36
WOR-TV, 6
WQXR Radio, 5
Wright, Teresa, 143
Wyndham Theater, 35
Xanadu, 99, 144
York, Susannah, 36
York Theater, 135
Young Actors Space, 144
Young, Gig, 36
Your Own Thing, 17
"Zip-a-Dee-Doo-Dah," 12

www.ingramcontent.com/pod-product-compliance
Lightning Source LLC
Chambersburg PA
CBHW051108160426
43193CB00010B/1360